The Participation Revolution

NEIL GIBB is a consultant, writer, speaker, and social advocate. He has spent his whole career looking at how new thinking and technology can be applied to improve business and society. Today he works with companies and organisations, helping them transform to thrive in the new economy. He also works with social enterprises, start-ups and recovery communities.

This book was a decade in the making, based on experience working in Europe, North America, Australia, Asia, and South America.

It's about transformation—about the emergence of a new social and economic paradigm.

It is designed as a manifesto for those who are out to change the world.

It provides a framework for transformation in the new economy.

And for anyone who might be interested, it shows you how to be a billionaire…in three easy moves.

The Participation Revolution

How to ride the waves of change
in a terrifyingly turbulent world

Neil Gibb

Published in 2018
by Eye Books
29A Barrow Street
Much Wenlock
Shropshire
TF13 6EN
www.eye-books.com

ISBN: 978-1-78563-055-2

Copyright © Neil Gibb 2017
All rights reserved.
The moral right of the author has been asserted.
No reproduction without permission.

Cover design by Heath Kane
Cover photograph by Bernie de Chant
Edited by John Ciavarella, Simon Edge, Clio Mitchell
Typeset by Clio Mitchell

www.neilgibb.com
www.transformation.ist

British Library Cataloguing in Publication Data
A catalogue record for this book is available from the British Library

Printed by CPI Group (UK) Ltd, Croydon CR0 4YY

I would like to acknowledge Eric Hutcheson, whose incredible life story, and mentoring, encouraged me to set off on the journey of discovery that led to this book. And Simon Fenton, whose friendship and support throughout my journey was so precious and who, tragically, died while the book was in preparation.

Thanks to Sarah Baxter, Sandy Rappaport, Robert Power, Mal Gibb, Josh Samuels, Nancy Nguyen, William Morgan, Kirsty Donovan, Erica Szabo, Nick Rimmer, Ed Tota, Julian Kell, Ira Rahmad, Philea Adhanti, Melody Briggs, Valeria Gonzales, Amanda Noga, Mei Lai Swan, Annie Belcher, Howard Johnson, Cindy Moussi, Christine Seale Nielsen and a whole load of other people I met along the way.

In memory of Simon Fenton (1970-2017)
Writer, explorer and pioneering
social entrepreneur

Prologue

Saturday 16 September 2008, Regents Street, London

The bright, hazy late-summer sun is beginning to dip in the sky, slanting a dark shadow across the elegant white-fronted Regency buildings that make up one of London's chicest retailing thoroughfares.

A rare balmy summer's day has bathed Regent Street in a dreamy, lazy ambience. On the wide pavements, the crowds have started to thin as afternoon cruises towards evening. People are meandering rather than the usual pushing and shoving.

About halfway down the west side of the street, in a patch still drenched in sunlight, there's a very different vibe. A scrum of people is pushing to enter a store-front door. It's a stark contrast to the relaxed feeling on the rest of the street. The expression on some of their faces is somewhere between panic and desperation.

This is the doorway to Apple's first flagship European store. The shop has been jammed with customers since it opened two years ago, but today it is particularly frenetic—the new iPhone 3 has just been released. Inside has the air of a fire sale. Sales assistants in blue T-shirts snake through the crowd, often with two or three customers vying for their attention.

Over by the iPhone demo area, a woman in her mid-30s is looking around frantically. She has been in the store for over half an hour, desperately trying to get the help of a sales assistant. Just as she is about to give up, and relinquish the demo model she is clutching, a thin young man emerges from the crowd, smiles, and starts to talk to her. Within minutes they are deep in conversation—she hanging on his every word, and he enthusiastically showing her how the phone works.

Across the street, things couldn't be more different. A hundred meters up towards Oxford Circus, a blue Nokia sign, lit by the late rays of the sun, hangs over a doorway that clearly doesn't have a scrum outside it. This is the home of Nokia's own new concept store. At a cost of over £4 million for its elegant fit-out alone, with a state-of-the-art translucent interactive wall, and a hip-looking lounge area, it's been designed to take the fight to Apple. Inside, good-looking, well-groomed, and well-trained assistants are aplenty. While Apple is a one-phone wonder, Nokia is the world's number one mobile phone maker. The racks in the store are resplendent with a range of cool-looking, well-designed smartphones, the top-end ones every bit as good as the iPhone in terms of functionality. What is more, Nokia has a proven track record in mobile communications and bulletproof reliability, while Apple is the new kid on the block with a somewhat patchy record when it comes to battery reliability in its smaller devices.

This should be a winning proposition.

But the Nokia store is practically empty. While customers in the Apple Store are pleading for sales assistants' attention, here they are acting far more consistent with the UK's cultural stereotype: friendly offers of help are at best met with a tight-lipped "No, thank you" and at worst by customers just marching out of the shop empty-handed.

By the end of 2009, with Apple's sales booming, and its stock price heading into outer space, new Apple Stores were popping up all around the world—each time heralded by the kind of mania that used to be reserved for pop bands like the Beatles.

Meanwhile, the Nokia flagship store on Regent Street quietly closed.

By 2012, Apple had displaced Exxon Mobil as the world's most valuable company. And in China, a particularly odd thing happened: a bunch of counterfeit Apple Stores were discovered. Yes, counterfeit stores—shops designed to look like Apple Stores. Everyone, it seemed, wanted a part of Apple.

Meanwhile, Nokia was a company in crisis. In April 2012, it announced it was cutting 7,000 of its workforce, and another 2,500 jobs were slashed later in the year.

The question on every analyst's lips was obvious: why did these two high-tech giants with equally fantastic products and reputations for innovation have such radically different fortunes?

People pointed to design, and leadership, and a whole host of other internal factors.

But they all missed a critical point.

The answer didn't lie inside the companies, but with that young man who approached the woman customer in the Regent Street Apple Store and started to help her with her phone. He wasn't an Apple sales assistant or employee—he was just a kid off the street; another shopper.

Why was it that in the Nokia store, where there were great products, free coffee, loads of space, and plenty of attentive sales assistants, customers were running out of the shop without a new phone, while in the crowded Apple Store other shoppers were actually prepared to help one another out?

In answering this question, we not only find what it takes to build successful businesses in the emerging new-world economic order, we actually have the answer to what it is going to take to successfully rebuild our societies in the networked age.

Contents

I. Introduction

When things fall apart	15
Disruption is the future calling	18
The great transformation	22
Creative destruction	26
How to use this book	29
The emergence of a new paradigm	31
That thing we seek	34
The rise of social economics	38
The participation revolution	49
Connected	61
Strategic shifts	71
The process of transformation	72
Architecture	74

II. Case stories

1. We are united!	77
2. The power of fans	86
3. How to be a billionaire in three easy moves: part 1	91
4. How to be a billionaire in three easy moves: part 2	99
5. Generation Why	108
6. Vision and blindness	116
7. Why we do what we do	124
8. In the club	132
9. The deadly serious game	146
10. How to be a billionaire in three easy moves: part 3	155

11. A higher calling	162
12. It ain't what you do, it's the why that you do it	173
13. The pursuit of happiness	181
14. Together	187
15. Home	194

III. How it works

Framework	205
1. Create a cause	207
A new kind of leadership	208
Bank to the future	213
The non-linear business model	217
2. Mobilise a movement	220
Weapons of mass participation	221
The art of transformation	224
Analytics and performance metrics	228
3. Build a community	231
Together	232
That thing we seek	236
Social economics	243

IV. Into action

A call to action	249
Manifesto	252
An open-source tool kit	253

"Tomorrow belongs to those who can hear it coming"

David Bowie

I. Introduction

When things fall apart

"You can't stop the waves, but you can learn to surf"

Jon Kabat-Zinn

Galileo Galilei was a clever lad. He is often referred to as the founding father of modern physics, of modern astronomy, of the scientific method, and of science itself. Einstein was one of his many fans.

Galileo was a geek, an engineer, a 16th-century hipster, *and* he could code. He was a pivotal figure in the great social and economic transformation that we now call the Renaissance. He was the inventor of one of the breakthrough technologies that enabled the discovery of the New World. He also played a pretty mean lute.

So influential was Galileo that, like Madonna and Prince, he was known simply by his first name.

But Galileo spent the latter part of his life under house arrest, having been very lucky to escape being executed in one of the many excruciating ways favoured by the inquisitions of the time.

The reason for this is worth remembering as we seek to navigate our way through a period of societal transformation very similar in scale and magnitude to the Renaissance.

Galileo said something that challenged the fundamental beliefs of the time—that the Sun, not Earth, was at the centre of the universe.

Like all great insights, it seems crazy with hindsight that people could be so resistant to something that now seems so obvious. It was a distinction that, once accepted, triggered one of the greatest periods of intellectual growth that mankind has ever experienced, critical to the development of navigation systems that allowed the New World to be discovered, and leading to a new system of logic, on which a whole new society and economy was built.

But it was something that, at the time, a lot of people just didn't want to hear—because people really don't like their beliefs to be challenged, even when all the signs are there that they are no longer working.

We are in the middle of a great transformation—a revolution that is blowing to bits beliefs, certainties, social systems and economic models that many of us had thought, and many still think, to be immutable and sacrosanct.

Now if that sounds a little dramatic, just take a look around. Political systems are breaking down, economic models are malfunctioning, opinion polls are no longer working, markets have become irrational, and once solid industries are being shaken apart. Everywhere, someone or something is disrupting, challenging and fundamentally changing how things are done.

At the same time, a social revolution is under way. Social media is dramatically reshaping the way we communicate, build relationships, and behave. Social conventions are being questioned and redrawn. Immigration and the movement of people on a scale never experienced before are putting cultures under huge pressure. National identities are being challenged, and individual certainties rocked to the core.

Across the globe, a cultural war has broken out—between progressives and conservatives, multi-culturalists and nationalists, atheists and those with faith, vegans and meat-eaters. It doesn't matter what the issue is, someone is shouting at someone.

Fear, anger, and conflict have become contagious.

When Pope Francis said, at a ceremony in Italy commemorating the centenary of First World War, that "perhaps one can speak of a third war, one fought piecemeal, with crimes, massacres, destruction," he put words to what a lot of people were feeling.

It can at times feel like everything is falling apart.

And there is a reason for this.

Because it is.

Disruption is the future calling

"It was the best of times, it was the worst of times, it was the age of wisdom, it was the age of foolishness, it was the epoch of belief, it was the epoch of incredulity, it was the season of Light, it was the season of Darkness, it was the spring of hope, it was the winter of despair, we had everything before us, we had nothing before us, we were all going direct to Heaven, we were all going direct the other way—in short, the period was so far like the present period, that some of its noisiest authorities insisted on its being received, for good or for evil, in the superlative degree of comparison only"

Charles Dickens, *A Tale of Two Cities*

On 11 March 1811, a small group of people started to congregate on the main street in Arnold, a leafy suburb on the edge of Nottingham in England. It was a cold, damp day, but the group grew quickly. A rebellious energy coursed through their ranks. They were not agitators by disposition. They were

Introduction 19

skilled workers from the local textile industry. But they were very angry.

The city's manufacturing companies were introducing radical new technologies and working practices that were disrupting their jobs and livelihoods beyond recognition. Skilled jobs were being lost to automation. Salaried jobs were being replaced with zero-hour contracts. Wages were falling, jobs were disappearing, people were being laid off. At the same time, local business owners were getting extremely rich.

On top of this, there was the shock of a new leader of what was then the world's most powerful nation—George IV, King of the United Kingdom. Whereas his predecessor, George III, had been a liberal, thoughtful man, popular with the people, George IV was brash, impulsive, and divisive. In the month since his inauguration, he had installed a bunch of his cronies in positions of power, subverting the normal mechanisms of government and making a series of seemingly alarming decisions.

It was just all too much. The small group was going to march on the city and mount a protest.

By the time it reached the city centre, its ranks had swollen into a huge indignant crowd. There were placards and angry speeches. A small faction broke away and marched on the factories in the Lace Market, breaking in and causing havoc.

The spontaneous uprising was contagious. Within a few days, much bigger protests had broken out in industrial cities across the country. Momentum grew. It was an insurgency that triggered mounting civil disorder—the largest protests the country had ever seen.

More than 200 years later, we call this group "Luddites", a movement that has become associated with resistance to change, people who are seen as being attached to old and outdated ways.

But at the time, that isn't what they were about. As far as the

Luddites were concerned, they were fighting against a society that seemed to be falling apart, they were fighting against chaos and collapse. Because what they couldn't see was the future.

The words "change" and "transformation" are often used interchangeably, but they mean very different things. Change is an orderly process: it is linear, predicable, and manageable. Transformation is a disruptive process: it is non-linear, challenging, and often quite traumatic.

Whereas the process of change is orderly, the process of transformation is highly disruptive. What is more, the greater the transformation, the greater the disruption leading up to it.

This is what the Luddites were experiencing.

Societal transformation has three distinct stages that bleed into one another, often with a great deal of turbulence as we move from one to the next.

It starts with an "enabling phase", a period that is triggered by the rapid emergence of some radical new technology that enables things to be done totally differently. In the Industrial Revolution, this technology was the steam engine and blast furnace, which enabled the mechanisation that the Luddites were protesting against.

And it ends with a "transformative phase", marked by the establishment of a new social, economic, and political paradigm— literally, a whole new set of rules, structures, systems, and social values. It was in this latter stage of the Industrial Revolution that the majority of the key social, political, and economic systems we have come to take for granted today were put in place: the Western democratic system, the abolition of slavery, the creation of the stock market, the corporation, running water, electric lighting, modern medicine, to name just a few.

In between these beginning and final phases is a difficult, uncomfortable, and increasingly unstable period of transition—

the "disruptive phase"—a turbulent and, for many people, traumatic phase, in which the old paradigm breaks down while the new one emerges. It is a period that when looked back on makes a great deal of sense, but at the time can just seem like everything is falling apart—and, of course, that is because everything is.

It was this increasingly disruptive and unsettling transitional phase that the Luddites were caught up in.

And it is the increasingly disruptive and unsettling transitional phase we are in now.

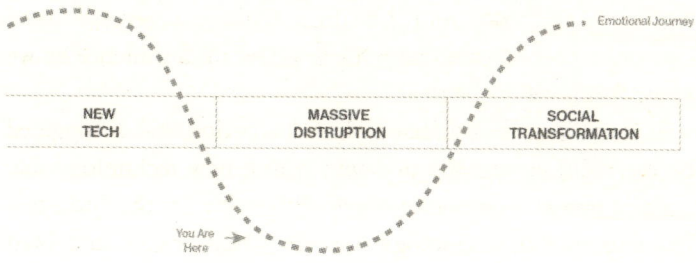

The great transformation

"Revolutions are inaugurated by a growing sense...that an existing paradigm has ceased to function adequately"

Thomas Kuhn, *The Structure of Scientific Revolutions*

Seventeen years after Sergey Brin and Larry Page first launched Google in their friend Susan Wojcicki's garage in Menlo Park, California, HBO released the second season of *Silicon Valley*, its fictional comedy parodying the thriving industry that had grown out of those early garage start-ups. In the third episode, Gareth Belson—CEO of a company that has more than a few parallels with the one that Brin and Page had created—rather grandiosely likened Silicon Valley to Europe in the Renaissance. It was said for comic effect, but like all great jokes, it was pretty close to the truth.

When John Watt and George White launched their start-up on the east side of the City of London in 1600, there were a lot of parallels with Silicon Valley in the late 1990s. The area around London docks had become a rabbit warren of little workshops, full of groups of twenty-something men hacking businesses together. Most of their meetings were done in the new hip coffee shops that were springing up around the area.

Introduction

And the whole thing was being financed by a network of private equity and venture capitalists. It was a hothouse of innovation, energy, and ambition.

Europe was in the throes of a massive transformation, driven by the emergence of two radical new enabling technologies: the movable type printing press had wrested control of the publishing and dissemination of information from the Roman Catholic Church, triggering an explosion of radical thinking and new ideas—it was the blogging platform of the early 1600s. And the development of precision systems meant that ships were suddenly able to venture way out beyond the horizon into "the New World", an innovation that was the era's GPS.

Buccaneering merchants were the high-tech entrepreneurs of the day, setting up high-risk but potentially super-high-return ventures to send ships into the New World and bring back exotic spices, materials and other goods.

Watt and White's vision was to create a supply line from Southeast Asia, a part of the world then known as the East Indies. Since branding wasn't yet a thing, they simply called their start-up "the East India Company".

The East India Company was the Amazon of the Renaissance, a business based on state-of-the-art logistics that quickly expanded way beyond its original remit. Very soon it was controlling the supply of goods from the whole of Asia.

Over the next 200 years, it grew and grew and grew. By 1780, the East India Company controlled more than half the world's trade. It was so influential that the founding fathers of the United States used its corporate flag as a template for The Stars and Stripes.

Then came the Industrial Revolution. The enabling phase of the Industrial Revolution empowered the East India Company in the same way the dot-com boom initially empowered incumbent businesses that had financial clout and infrastructure. But as the enabling phase gave way to disruption, the East India Company started to struggle. Like many corporations today, its growth started to stagnate and its profits declined. New start-ups with wild new ways of doing things came at it from all angles.

And by the time disruption gave way to transformation, the East India Company was no more. A mighty organisation that had controlled more than half the world's trade had become a footnote in history. To put that into context, it's like 90 percent of the current top 500 companies on the New York, Tokyo and London stock exchanges ceasing to exist in 20 years' time.

This might seem like a crazy notion, but that is what transformation looks like.

When things start to fall apart, there are two ways we can relate to them: as the end of something or the beginning of something.

There is a lot being written about the system that is breaking down, ideas and theories about what needs to happen to fix it. People are getting angrier, trying to resist. There is a lot of effort being put into shoring it up and trying to stop it falling apart.

History tells us, though, that resistance is futile. That is what the Luddites and the East India Company show us.

So this book isn't about any of that. It isn't about the rights and wrongs of what is happening, whose fault it is, or what could and should be done to fix it. It is about transformation and how to transform, how to step into the future, how to thrive in the rapidly emerging new economic order. It isn't for those who want to hang on to the world as it was—it is for those who want to learn how to flourish in the world as it is becoming.

In short, the book is a manifesto for those who really are out to change the world—to create the political parties of tomorrow, the social systems, the new businesses, new jobs, new fuels and, perhaps most importantly, the new societies.

It is also a framework for the transformation of existing businesses and enterprises to thrive in the new economic order; how to pivot, realign and genuinely innovate.

And, lastly, for anyone who might be interested, it shows how to be a billionaire…in three easy moves.

Creative destruction

"Every act of creation is first an act of destruction"

Pablo Picasso

In 1942 the Austrian-American economist Joseph Schumpeter popularised the concept of "creative destruction", describing it as the "process of industrial mutation that incessantly revolutionises the economic structure from within, incessantly destroying the old one, incessantly creating a new one." Schumpeter's point is that every act of creation, and every act of groundbreaking innovation, however good and useful they are, is also an act of destruction, in that it supplants something. Thus the automobile destroyed demand for the horse-drawn carriage, digital photography for film, Netflix for video stores, and the iPhone for a whole host of things.

Creative destruction tends to a maximum in periods of societal transformation such as the present one. Everything is up for grabs, and everything is at risk. In the next 10 to 20 years the chances are that 70 percent of current jobs will most likely no longer exist. Whereas the industrial revolution replaced skilled manual labour, digitisation and increasingly intelligent algorithms are replacing middle management and white collar jobs. Industries like banking, oil and gas, law, accountancy, pharmaceuticals, healthcare, education and logistics will be turned on their heads. Many, many of today's large corporations will simply cease to be.

What the Luddites showed is that resistance is futile, but that doesn't make what happened to them any less traumatic. We become attached to things, especially professions, business models and institutions that have been with us all our lives. The reason large incumbent corporations and industries so often fail in times of structural change is because there is a collective unconscious belief that the underlying fundamentals of their businesses are immutable. But as the fall of the once all-powerful East India Company shows, when the social and economic paradigm tips, things change fast. The people and companies that will thrive in the new economic order are those who are able to act early.

Because of this, I have worked hard to stay objective. I have chosen some case studies and examples that may not sit well with how you want the world to be—in some cases they don't with mine, either. But I include them, as they illustrate emerging phenomena most clearly. The point of doing this is not to celebrate them but to give us choice. Denial is perhaps our most dangerous human characteristic, especially when things suddenly change. It works to protect us in the short term from unpalatable truths, but often opens us up to huge downstream risk.

My view is that by distinguishing how things work, independently of whether we like how they are being applied or not, we give ourselves the opportunity to take the insight, and apply it in ways that make the world work in a way that we want. And that, really, is my goal here. To provide the means to be on the front foot, to surf change, to shape the future, not just to survive, but to thrive in the rapidly emerging new social and economic order.

There are many ways the future can go. There are certainly some dark and dystopian scenarios possible if we don't collectively act. But I believe we also have at our fingertips the means to create a new golden age for humanity—a world that really does work for everyone. And that is what I am interested in.

The game is on. Which is why this book is really an invitation.

How to use this book

"We are called to be architects of the future, not its victims"

R Buckminster Fuller

1. A manifesto for those who are out to change the world
2. A framework for transformation in the new economy
3. How to be a billionaire—in three easy moves

Books are pretty old tech. The basic structure of the modern book goes back to the invention of bookbinding and the printing press. Back then, things were developed in a linear fashion, with a beginning, a middle, and an end. The book had to be a discrete package. There was no Internet to cross-reference, no background of always-on media. So books were designed to be worked through in an orderly fashion.

We don't live in a world like that anymore, though. So I have structured this book in a different way.

In this first section, I provide a complete summary. If you want to understand the key themes and then use the model, it is all here.

In the second section, I share case stories that step through how my thinking evolved—this is both the research and the evidence. My insight didn't come from book or online research, although I did a lot of that to back up what I saw. It was developed out of extensive on-the-ground exploration and experimentation. I was aware that a lot of modern business and social research is kind of self-referential, research based on research, and it is also very Western-centric. So, during the course of my research, I spent a protracted period in the field in Asia, the Middle East, and South America, as well as North America, Australia, and Europe—an approach I call "deep hanging out".

In the third section, I lay out a framework for transformation—this is the place to look for tips on implementation. What I present is a tried-and-tested framework, not a theory. It was developed in the field of play, in corporations, start-ups, and social enterprises.

Finally, in the fourth section, I boil it all down to its very essence—what Putri and her friends, whose story I share here, would call "the skinny". A manifesto, a tool kit, and a set of distinctions to work with. I don't in any way claim this to be a *fait accompli*. It is the beginnings of a conversation—a starting point. I have therefore made all the material available online in an open-source Google doc, to share, add to, develop, and build on.

The emergence of a new paradigm

"When things are shaky and nothing is working, we might realise that we are on the verge of something. We might realise that this is a very vulnerable and tender place, and that tenderness can go either way. We can shut down and feel resentful or we can touch in on that throbbing quality"

Pema Chödrön

The Guardian, 20 July 2016
"The International Monetary Fund has slashed its forecast for UK growth next year after warning that the decision to leave the EU had damaged the British economy's short-term prospects and 'thrown a spanner in the works' of the global recovery."

The Guardian, 4 October 2016
"The International Monetary Fund has predicted the UK will be the fastest growing of the G7 leading industrial countries this year and accepted that its prediction of a post-Brexit-vote financial crash proved to be overly pessimistic…it stuck to its view that the economy would eventually suffer from the shock

EU referendum result, and said expansion next year would be just 1.1%."

The Guardian, 16 January 2017
"The International Monetary Fund has upgraded its forecasts for the UK economy this year after the latest signs that businesses and consumers have shrugged off the Brexit vote... The IMF forecast that the UK will grow by 1.5% this year, up from a previous estimate of 1.1%."

On 6 January 2017, Andy Haldane, the chief economist at the Bank of England, made a stark admission. "The economics profession is to some degree in crisis," he admitted, in a speech to the Institute for Government.

What he was referring to was the Bank of England's abject failure either to foresee the global financial crisis or to accurately assess the economic impact of the UK's decision to leave the European Union. In both cases, it seemed to have been blindsided.

Now if these two chronic mis-assessments had been isolated incidents, maybe we could have shrugged them off as a couple of bad days at the office.

But the crisis Haldane was referring to was far bigger than just a couple of big miscalculations. In fact, it was far bigger than economics. What he was pointing to was a seeming breakdown in forecasting and expert opinion across the board.

In May 2015, a whole raft of formerly reliable opinion polls had predicted a close-fought general election in the UK. In the weeks running up to the election, two of the three major polls had suggested the Labour opposition party would have a narrow victory. Right up to the close of voting, the polls were saying it would be neck-and-neck. But they were spectacularly wrong. The ruling Conservative Party routed Labour, winning by nearly 100 parliamentary seats.

A year later came the referendum on the UK's membership in the EU. Once again, reliable opinion polls got it wrong, causing perhaps the greatest spillage of *chai lattes* in urban liberal enclaves ever seen.

Then there were the economic forecasts from both the Bank of England and the International Monetary Fund—surely, *the* experts in all things economic—in the aftermath.

The IMF's gloomy post-referendum forecast turned out to be way off the mark. Instead of going down as predicted, property prices went up. Instead of stuttering, growth was strong.

Three months later, the IMF hastily revised its prediction. But again, it was wrong. In early 2017, it had to admit its second forecast had also turned out to be incorrect and tried again.

This was set against a backdrop of all sorts of other confusion. Inflation was supposed to go up, but it didn't. The rapid decline in oil prices was meant to be good news, but the drop seemed anything but.

In the meantime, the biggest shock of all had happened. On Tuesday 8 November 2016, Donald Trump was elected president of the United States, defying every major poll, metric, tracker, expert opinion, and analysis. No one called it—not even the outliers who make their reputations on calling such things.

People started to panic. What on earth was going on?

That thing we seek

"I define connection as the energy that exists between people when they feel seen, heard, and valued; when they can give and receive without judgment; and when they derive sustenance and strength from the relationship"

Dr. Brené Brown

Breakthroughs happen in the most unlikely places, at the most unlikely times. And sometimes with the most unlikely people.

Mine came with Carlo—former drug dealer who had been incarcerated at age 19 for beating a man half to death—as we watched from a hill while the setting sun cast a beautiful pink glow across Echo Park, a Latino neighbourhood on the north side of Central Los Angeles.

Carlo worked for a social enterprise called Homeboy Industries, which I had decided to look up while I was in town. Homeboy was set up just after the LA riots in 1992, by Father Gregory Boyle, a Jesuit priest. Its mission is to rehabilitate kids from the gangs—help them get clean, get trained, get back into work. Carlo was one of those kids.

When I met him, he had been clean for a couple of years. Homeboy had helped him manage his anger and remove his gang tattoos. He was in a training program to get into video production, but he still had a long way to go. He was back living with his parents, working three poorly paid jobs to pay off various debts and fines. He still couldn't get to see his kid.

But he was a man on a mission. He made a stark contrast to some of the executives I had been working with earlier in the day. They were good people, well-paid, working for a cash-rich company, but still, there was something in the background I found hard to put words to. It might best be described as a kind of spiritual weariness. The whole experience had felt a little like wading through invisible mud.

Carlo was a man with no money, working minimum wage with all sorts of challenges. But he had that thing, that glow, that sense of hope and possibility that we all want.

So I asked him, "What was it about Homeboy that had made such a difference?"

He thought for a moment.

"Because I feel connected," he said, for the first time all day his expression suddenly serious. "You know, to something that is meaningful and matters. Something that is real. Homeboy's given me purpose. A place I belong. I know they got my back. I ain't ever had that before."

In 2011, the American Career Advisory Board ran the largest study of its kind, designed to understand the career aspirations of the generation that was coming to be called the millennials. What they found was a marked difference between the perception that older managers held about this generation and the actual views of the so-called millennials themselves. While the managers said that money and status were the main drivers for the younger generation, the younger people surveyed unequivocally pointed to something else, something far more crucial and interesting.

We are in the middle of a great transformation, a

transformation that marks the emergence of a new social and economic paradigm. Political systems are breaking down. Productivity is flat-lining in corporations. Engagement in many traditional businesses remains stubbornly elusive. Economic indicators and measures are no longer making sense.

It is a transformation that, like the Renaissance and Industrial Revolution, is being enabled by new technology. In this case, digital technology.

But that is not what this transformation is about.

Three-quarters of those between 21 and 31 years old surveyed in 2011 said that having a career with a sense of purpose and meaning was most important to them.

And since then, study after study has amplified this finding in different ways. More importantly, so have the social trends. Analysis of the millennial mindset has tended to associate it with a specific age range, but generational change is actually about a shift in our collective consciousness. It just starts with the young because they are the ones who always bring in change—because societal and cultural change doesn't come from the top down, it always emerges from the bottom up.

The global financial crisis was the explosion in the old system that blew cracks into its foundations, cracks that have spread and spread.

And what is now emerging is a new social and economic model with a whole new set of rules.

"See that?" Carlo asked me, pointing at the pink haze that hung across the valley. "You know what that is?"

"The haze?"

"Yeah, the haze," he laughed, mimicking my English accent. "What do you think it is?"

"It's pollution," I said. "From the traffic."

"Nah. That's what everyone says, because that's what everyone gets told. But it ain't. That pink is the dust off the desert. It's real. When you know that, it changes everything."

The rise of social economics

1. Generation why

"Facebook was not originally created to be a company. It was built to accomplish a social mission—to make the world more open and connected"

Mark Zuckerberg, Facebook

When Sergey Brin and Larry Page first set-up Google in a friend's garage in Menlo Park in the autumn of 1998, they were very clear why they were doing it: "to organise the world's information and make it universally accessible and useful."

They also had a great tool to achieve this: a search engine they had developed while they were PhD students, which used very different algorithms to any other on the market.

What they didn't have, though, was a means to generate revenue. Other search engines had the same challenge, and the received wisdom of the time was that the best way to make money would be to game the results—charge businesses to knock their results up the listings.

Brin and Page refused to do this, though. Theirs was a social mission, something that they cared deeply about. And it was something they weren't prepared to sell out on.

But there was more to what Brin and Page were up to than good intention. What they were actually doing was applying a new kind of logic, a system of thinking and ethics that would empower the emergence of a whole new economic paradigm.

In the 1970s, a new form of mathematics began to emerge. Quantum mechanics, chaos theory and systems theory all combined into a new form of non-linear mathematics—a system of logic that underpinned the development of the digital technology and networks that businesses like Google, Apple, Facebook and the tech companies that are now transforming our societies are based on. It is binary logic, not analogue, and it is about holistic systems, rather than granular units.

As computational scientists, Brin and Page understood the concept of "systemic integrity". Either a system could be trusted or it could not. So, for them, their social mission wasn't just some noble intention or sales tool that could be taken or left; it was fundamental to how the system worked. It was something that had to come before everything else.

This was a 'sun is the centre of the universe' assertion—a radical hypothesis that would become the fundamental principle of a new social and economic system.

But for a lot of people—especially the advertising industry—it was something they really couldn't get their heads around.

The mercantile economic system that propelled the East India Company to world domination was based on moving things from one part of the world to another, where they could be sold for more. Coffee would be grown in Indonesia using "indentured labour" (a historically euphemistic term for what was essentially a form of slavery). It was then moved to the Netherlands, where it was sold to the new, wealthy middle classes of Europe for much more. The power in this system lay with the merchants.

The Industrial Revolution replaced the mercantile system with what would become the consumer economic system. In this model, value was created by selling things for more than they cost to make. The power in this system lay initially with the factory owners and then with the brand and intellectual property owners as the model matured. As it entered its end game in the late 1990s, the power shifted to those who simply traded in stock. The global financial crisis was the sign that this system was beginning to fail.

What both these systems had in common, though, was that they worked for the seller. This was so fundamental it was impossible for most people to consider anything else.

But what Brin and Page did, by applying the principle of systemic integrity, was put Google on the side of the user.

Now at first read, it could be easy just to shrug this off and point out that many businesses have always worked for their customers.

But this is far more fundamental than that. Remember—Galileo, Galileo, Galileo!

Being on the side of the user doesn't mean being customer-centric or user-focused. It means literally on the side of the user. Over there, with them. Working with their best interests as your primary focus. Often to the detriment of those who are selling products or services.

This is the emerging new economic paradigm, and the high-growth new businesses are the ones that are applying it.

In the consumer economic model, music companies focused on making and selling music. In the social economic model, Spotify focuses on the fulfilment of a social mission: "to give people access to all the music they want all the time—in a completely legal and accessible way." Spotify is on the side of

Introduction

the user—those who want to access and listen to music—not those who are selling it.

In the consumer economic model, taxi and transportation companies focused on generating revenue from their vehicles and fleets. In the social economic model, Uber focuses on the fulfilment of a social mission: "to make transport as reliable as running water". It is out to get the best deal for the traveller.

And in the consumer economic model, oil and gas companies focused on finding and selling hydrocarbons. In the social economic model, Tesla is focused on the fulfilment of a social mission: "to accelerate the world's transition to sustainable energy".

This is what distinguishes social economics from consumer economics. It is focused on the *why*, not the *what*; it works on behalf of the user, not the seller; and it has a singleness of purpose—the fulfilment of a social mission.

Applying the principles of social economics enabled Google not so much to disrupt the advertising industry as to blow it to pieces. The advertising industry worked on behalf of sellers, and over the years, had developed more and more cunning ways to coerce and manipulate people into desiring and buying things. Google went to work on behalf of its users, essentially preventing the advertising industry from doing that. It created a very clear demarcation between its system and any commercial advertising, putting the wants and needs of its users above everything else.

In 1999, Google's revenues were $200,000. Two years later, they had increased to more than $700 million.

Ten years after Brin and Page first moved Google into the garage in Menlo Park, the company's revenues hit $21 billion.

By 2018, they will exceed $100 billion. This is the power of social economics.

2. Your stand is your brand

"I grew up in a society where everything you did was eavesdropped on, recorded, snitched on. Nobody should have the right to eavesdrop, or you become a totalitarian state—the kind of state I escaped as a kid to come to this country where you have democracy and freedom of speech. Our goal is to protect it"

Jan Koum, WhatsApp

Jan Koum was like a lot of immigrant kids who are born in one country and brought up in another—he had a foot in both cultures. Like Sergey Brin at Google, he was born in what was then the Soviet Union, and moved to the United States as a kid. Like Brin, he was also Jewish. This meant he had been born into a culture where he knew what it was like to be snooped on and oppressed.

In 2009, Koum saw Apple's newly launched App Store and had an idea. He got together with a couple of friends and they started to hack together a messaging app.

There were already a lot of ways for people to communicate electronically with each other, and new messaging apps were already popping up on the App Store. This, though, is where Koum's background was important.

Koum took a stand. He didn't just want to build a messenger app, he wanted to provide the means for people to have the freedom to communicate with each other without the possibility of any snooping or outside interference—and that didn't just mean from governments and other agencies, but from advertisers, too.

Koum decided to call their messenger "WhatsApp."

WhatsApp's purpose was the fulfilment of a very clear social mission: to provide the means for people to communicate with each other without being snooped on. Like Google, its allegiances were firmly on the side of its user. All messages would be encrypted, and no data would be collected, stored, or used.

This flew in the face of the prevailing view of the day, which said that personal data was where the money was.

But Koum was having none of it. He understood the principle of systemic integrity. He understood on a personal level why this was a binary proposition. It only took one slip in the Soviet Union to find yourself in a prison cell, and one slip in America to have people calling you day and night trying to sell you life insurance. A system either worked or it didn't, and he became obsessed with making sure WhatsApp was bulletproof.

A beta version of the app was launched in June 2009—and quickly gained more than 200,000 users. A movement began to build from the ground up, especially in countries with oppressive regimes. Trust is transactional—and in a network, it multiplies. As news stories started to surface about Western governments' surveillance of electronic communications, WhatsApp's user base quickly grew.

We can sniff out authenticity; we can feel it. Like Brin and Page, what drove Koum wasn't the desire to create an app, to become a billionaire, or a love of tech, although these might all have been in the mix. What drove him was that his social mission was something meaningful that mattered to him a lot. It was authentic. It was, as Carlo said of Homeboy, *real*. Koum connected with it at a very deep and emotional level.

Koum's stand became WhatsApp's brand. People knew they could rely on it. They knew they wouldn't get a call in the night from a call centre in India pretending to be offering a Windows upgrade, or from the secret police.

In an era of escalating disruption and ever-increasing change, if you hang on to what you do you get left behind. Why, though, creates a context in which innovation can occur. The bigger the why, the more meaningful and real it is for those involved—the bigger the impact.

On 19 February 2014, Facebook bought WhatsApp for $19 billion, the largest sum ever paid for what was essentially still a start-up.

By the end of 2016, more than 1.2 billion people were regularly using WhatsApp to communicate with each other—one in six of the world's population.

3. We are the customer

"I didn't know anything about garments, didn't know anything about running retail, or running online retail. And I had never set up my own brand before. So there was a lot to learn and a lot of risk. But the key thing is it came out of me being the customer. You understand the customer, because you *are* the customer"

Simon Mottram, founder and CEO, Rapha

In the summer of 2002, Nick Woodman arrived in Bali to surf. Woodman was nursing his wounds after the failure of his marketing business back in California, and he had gone to Indonesia to clear his head and have some fun.

As much as Woodman wanted to get away from all it all, he still had that exhibitionist streak that most surfers have. He didn't just want to ride the waves, he wanted his friends and others to see what he was up to.

A cottage video industry had grown up in Bali, but Woodman was unimpressed—while a video shot from the beach captured a sense of the awe of surfing, it didn't really capture the experience.

He therefore decided to take matters into his own hands. He strapped a 35mm film camera in a plastic bag to one hand and set off into the waves. The results were not great.

But the game was on. Woodman started to experiment. He got feedback from other surfers in the cafés and bars he hung out in, and tried again.

Woodman called his fledgling brand "GoPro." He didn't have any experience or background in making cameras or tech. He didn't have any labs or experts working with him. At one point, he and his wife sold bangles made out of shells by the roadside in California to raise funds.

But what he did have was a social mission. He had a why, not a what. As a surfer, he was instinctively on the side of the user. He had a singleness of purpose—he was determined to develop the best means to share his high-octane experiences with others in the simplest and most accessible way possible. This was what drove his design thinking.

Industries that think in terms of "consumers" become preoccupied with stoking desires and cravings. Theirs becomes a game of manipulation and coercion.

Companies that think in terms of "customers" become preoccupied with their products and services. It becomes all about what they source, make and sell.

Teams that think in terms of "users" have a far more human focus, but their preoccupation tends toward the functional. It becomes about tech and interaction.

But when we make our focus the fulfilment of a social mission, like Woodman did, we intuitively start to think in terms of the "whole human experience": functional, emotional, social—spiritual.

It was on the beaches of Bali, retracing Woodman's steps, hanging out with surfers, and falling in the water a lot, that I began to really understand the source of the innovation that is transforming our society, and in so doing, creating a new breed of high-growth businesses.

Indonesia played a critical part in the social and economic transformation of the Renaissance, as the Dutch colonised it and made it the centre of the world's coffee production. For more than 300 years, bar four years of British rule, Indonesia was run by the Dutch. Today, though, apart from a few canals and old buildings, there is very little left behind. It was an extractive process, designed to make the merchants who were trading the coffee rich.

In 1995, Clayton Christensen, a professor at the Harvard Business School, introduced the term "disruptive innovation" in his book *The Innovator's Dilemma*. As the twin forces of digital technology and globalisation have shaken up and disrupted just about every aspect of our lives in the 21st century, disruptive innovation has become the rallying cry of a generation. Disruption, we are told, is the source of breakthroughs, transformation, and spectacular success.

But when I tracked back to the source of innovation of the so-called disruptive companies like GoPro, what I found had nothing to do with disruption. Disruption was simply a side effect.

As I travelled through Indonesia, I noticed keenly the effect that social media and digital tools were having on its culture. Many young people under the age of 35, especially in the capital city of Jakarta, speak perfect English, often with a Californian lilt, picked up from being brought up with access to YouTube, TMZ, and BuzzFeed. They are switched on, savvy, and socially connected via Instagram, Snapchat, and Path. These new tools and platforms are not disruptive; they are participatory. They enable people to participate more fully in society, life, things they need to do, activities they are passionate about.

Ten years after Woodman first waded into the water in Bali with a camera in a plastic bag strapped to his hand, GoPro replaced Sony as the best-selling digital imaging camera at American retailer Best Buy—the first time Sony had been usurped in the chain's history—having totally transformed how video content was made, viewed, and shared.

GoPro had certainly disrupted the digital video industry.

But what had made GoPro so successful wasn't that it was disruptive—that was just the side effect. GoPro was the product of "participatory innovation". It made it easy to participate and take part.

This is the source of the success of the fast-growing businesses and movements in the emerging new economy.

Google applied the principles of participatory innovation. Brin and Page focused their attention on how to make it easier for people to participate in finding reliable information, in finding things without being gamed by advertisers. Google connects its users to people, information, and things. It makes it easy to participate in life.

Koum applied the principles of participatory innovation—making it easier, safer, and cheaper to participate in communicating with others. WhatsApp makes it easier to participate in society.

Woodman applied the principles of participatory innovation. GoPro makes it easier to participate in sharing our experiences.

The impact of participatory innovation is profound. It is enabling a structural shift in how our societies and economies work—from passive consumption to active participation.

The consumer economic model generates value from selling products and services. In the emerging social economic model, value is generated by enabling participation. Consumers are replaced by participants, customers by enthusiasts and fans.

In December 2012, Taiwanese electronic giant Foxconn paid $200 million for 8.88 percent of GoPro, making Woodman, who owned the majority of the stock, a paper billionaire. Eighteen months later, GoPro went public, valuing the company at $3 billion and making Woodman an actual billionaire.

In 2013, the high-tech investor Aileen Lee coined the term "unicorn" in an article in *TechCrunch* magazine, referring to a new breed of companies that rapidly grow to a billion-dollar valuation. It was a beautiful and brilliant metaphor, pointing to the seemingly magical nature of these companies.

The magic, though, isn't something mystical and esoteric.

When *TechCrunch* published a list of the most valuable unicorns in early 2017, the top five were all participatory innovations. Uber (founded 2009, value $62.5 billion), Didi Chuxing (founded 2012, value $50 billion), and Airbnb (founded 2008, value $31 billion) are participatory platforms. Ant Financial (founded 2010, value $60 billion) is a participatory tool, enabling users to participate safely in China's burgeoning e-commerce markets. Xiaomi (founded 2010, value $45 billion) is a participatory brand, crowd-sourcing users to participate in the design process as a means to make smartphones available at as near the cost of production as possible.

The participation revolution

1. Everyone will be famous for 15 people

"Music itself is going to become like running water or electricity... So it's like, just take advantage of these last few years because none of this is ever going to happen again. You'd better be prepared for doing a lot of touring because that's really the only unique situation that's going to be left. It's terribly exciting. But on the other hand it doesn't matter if you think it's exciting or not; it's what's going to happen"

David Bowie, 1999

Rik looks like he might be a member of the Red Hot Chili Peppers, but it turns out he is actually a neurosurgeon. As our drinks arrive at the café, he gets a call. He talks quickly, then pulls out an iPad. I notice, as the server places his macadamia nut smoothie on the table, that he is looking at a brightly coloured image of a brain.

I am in the middle an experiment. One of the fundamental design principles I applied as I developed the thinking I share in this book is the principle of heuristic research—in plain English, this means "trial-and-error development in the real world". Throughout my career, I have worked with a lot of teams doing "user research". We built profiles and complex journeys and all sorts of good stuff. But what was notable looking back was how rarely we went deep into the field, essentially meaning that a lot of what we were creating was at best an abstraction and in many cases wishful thinking. You can spend as much time as you like nuancing "Jenny", 35, who lives in Brighton, loves yoga, and is interested in organic products. But if she ain't real, she won't be jumping through the hoops your design team wants her to.

The café is the meeting place for a group that is on its way to the Coachella Valley Music and Arts Festival 130 miles east of Los Angeles. It's a groovy little spot, roughly halfway between LA and the Southern Californian city of Indio, where the festival is held. The meet-up emerged out of an online discussion thread I joined about the festival.

The experiment I am conducting is to see if I can do the whole trip using participatory tools on my iPhone. I found my accommodation using Airbnb. I booked my flight using a budget air travel app. I used Uber to get to the airport. I arranged a rideshare at the other end on the groups' Facebook event page. I used Apple maps and WhatsApp to arrange a place to meet. In the half hour since we arrived at the café, I have posted three moody photos of palm trees to Instagram to prove to my friends what a groovy time I am having, responded to an important email from a client, and checked the weather. I think I am doing pretty well.

When Rik gets off his call, I ask him if he is OK. He nods and beams: "Yep, I think we just did a good day's work."

He tells me that his area of expertise is something he calls "brain reanimation". I have to admit that up until this point, I hadn't known that brain reanimation was a thing—but apparently it is. He explains that when someone has a stroke, some of the brain will be irreparably damaged, and some of it remains unaffected. But often there is also some tissue that, if a neurosurgeon like Rik can get to it quickly enough, can be reanimated—coaxed back to life. When a stroke hits, there is a very small window of opportunity though which something can be done. The hospital Rik works in is a seven-hour drive away, so there is no way he could get back in time. Using the iPad, he is able to give his colleagues support and act as a second viewpoint.

"So you mean you just did brain surgery? " I ask.

"Yes," Rik says, taking a long pull on his smoothie.

When I glance at my iPhone, there are three red notification icons showing, but somehow they don't seem quite as pressing as they might have done five minutes earlier. Instead, I go to Google and type in "brain reanimation".

In the autumn of 2007, Madonna Louise Ciccone did what she has been doing her entire career. She made a move that at the time raised a few eyebrows but with hindsight would turn out to be a signifier of change.

Madonna the performer has always been a keen reader of emerging social trends, very rapidly assimilating them into her act, and in so doing, bringing new ideas to the mainstream. It is what consistently keeps her ahead of the curve.

But two things distinguished her 2007 move as particularly significant. First, it was a business, not an artistic, decision. And second, rather than heralding a passing fashion or trend, it marked the emergence of a new social and economic system.

Madonna signed her first record deal with the Warner Music

Group in 1982. Her eponymous debut album, launched the following year, sold over 10 million copies worldwide, blasting her to international stardom. Over the next 25 years, she sold over 200 million units on Warner-owned labels.

In 2007, it was time for a contract renewal, and this is where she made what, at the time, seemed to many to be a strange move. She had two big offers on the table. The first was a generous new deal from Warner Brothers to continue their highly successful relationship, a relationship that gave Madonna a lot of autonomy and power. The second was from a relatively new company called Live Nation. What was particularly interesting about Live Nation was that it wasn't a record company, it was a live events company. It had no track record at all in making and selling records. Given that this is how Madonna had been making a very tidy living for the past 25 years, Live Nation didn't seem an obvious fit.

Professor Colin Barrow at Cranfield School of Management in England has described Madonna as "America's smartest business woman". It was during her contract negotiations that she showed it.

Instead of re-signing with Warner Brothers, she signed with Live Nation.

Emergence takes time. The people who are most successful in life are the ones who catch the swell early. It's one thing I learned retracing Nick Woodman's steps in Bali. The best surfers are the ones who seem to be able to spot a wave just before it starts to rise.

What Madonna was responding to were the early signs of a structural shift in how our economy works, from a model where value is generated from passive consumption—in the case of the music industry, this was buying records, CDs, and MP3s—to a model where value is generated from active participation.

In 1997, Paul Tollet visited the Glastonbury Festival in the UK. Tollet was a music promoter from LA, and what he experienced at Glastonbury was very different from the kind of large-scale gigs he'd been involved with back home. Rather than a crowd of people watching bands, Glastonbury was a huge communal experience, of which music seemed to be just one part.

Two years later, Tollet launched the first Coachella Valley Music and Arts Festival. The event had seven main acts and attracted a very healthy 37,000 people.

By 2007, Coachella had been extended from two days to three, and attendance had grown to 187,000. More crucially, it had morphed and developed, based on what Tollet had experienced at Glastonbury. As well as bands, there were arts. There were crafts. Chill-out tents. Yoga. There was even a giant snowball fight—quite a bizarre experience in an area that is essentially a desert. The festival was no longer just about watching people play, it was about being actively involved.

Businesses that base their thinking on the notion of "the consumer" talk about "shifts in consumer sentiment". It is impossible to understand the shift in a paradigm, though, using the thinking that generated the existing paradigm.

What we are seeing is not a shift in consumer sentiment, it is a shift in human sentiment. The concept of "the consumer" is an abstraction, a distinction designed to dehumanise the people that companies are targeting. What we are now experiencing is the end of the feeding frenzy that is the end game of consumerism, and the rise of a new paradigm—one in which passive consumers are replaced by active participants. This is the really big deal.

In 2016, the Coachella Valley Economic Partnership and Greater Palm Springs Convention and Visitors Bureau published their joint findings on the economic impact of the 2015

Coachella Music and Arts Festival on the area. In total, the 2015 festival generated $704 million in an ecosystem of businesses—from the promoters and acts, to transportation, catering, hotels and local jobs; this is the equivalent of five percent of global music sales from just one festival.

The rise of mass-participation festivals like Coachella, and the many others that have expanded rapidly all over the globe, coincided with the emergence of a whole series of tools and platforms enabling the mass-participation of making and sharing music, too. Apple Macs running packages like GarageBand and Logic Pro. iTunes. MySpace. YouTube. Suddenly, something that had once been scarce and difficult to do was available to everyone.

This triggered a revolution.

In 1968, the American pop artist Andy Warhol, whose work both fetishised and celebrated consumerism, famously said, "In the future, everyone will be famous for 15 minutes."

The social economy offers a new possibility: that in the future, everyone will be famous for 15 people.

In 2008, the music streaming service Spotify launched, completing this shift of value generation in the music business from product to participation.

Spotify's primary purpose is the fulfilment of a social mission: "to give people access to all the music they want all the time—in a completely legal and accessible way." There's no what—just a why. It works on behalf of the user, not the seller. And it enables participation. The result is that it takes scarcity out of the system, increasing the value of the overall system from the user's perspective, and in so doing, reducing the cost of individual interactions.

In early 2017, the singer Ed Sheeran clocked up more than 273 million streams on Spotify for his album *Divide* in just seven days—a new record for the platform. Spotify pays around $0.005 per play. Peanuts when only a few hundred people listen to your music. But when you are Ed Sheeran, assuming everyone listened to all 12 tracks of the album, it generated $16.5 million

This is how the participation revolution works: revenue is generated from participation, not from the sale of a song or product. The value to the user is the system, not the individual parts.

The participation revolution signifies a structural shift in how our societies and economies work—a shift from passive consumption to active participation. To thrive in this new emerging economy requires a shift in commercial mindset from how to generate value from products to how to generate value from participatory experiences.

In 2016, sponsorship of live music events in the United States exceeded $2 billion. The performer Taylor Swift generated $17 per person from merchandising at her live events. While these were physical items, they were items that augmented the participatory experience, rather than the other way around.

The fast-growing brands that make some kind of physical items in the new economy are participatory—they make tools rather than products. Lulu Lemon doesn't make fashion items, it makes clothing and apparel that enable people to participate in yoga. It supports yoga teachers, and sponsors and hosts classes and events. The brand adds to and improves the experience of participating in yoga. The road cycling brand Rapha doesn't just make great-looking cycling clothing and accessories, it makes items that enable participation in the sport of hard-core road cycling. It sponsors cycling teams, and hosts an ongoing series of participatory events and rides around the world. Everything it does is about enabling fans and enthusiasts to participate in hard-core road cycling. If you work at Rapha, you ride a bike.

These are not consumer brands, they are participatory brands.

The participation revolution is changing how we work and make money, shifting the value from those who sell products and provide services to those who enable participation. It will have the same effect on a lot of working people as mechanisation had on the Luddites, and it will have the same effect on corporations as the Industrial Revolution had on the East India Company.

The power in this new emerging economic model lies with those who broker and enable connections between people, experiences, and things: the participatory toolmakers like WhatsApp and GoPro, the participatory platforms like YouTube and Spotify, and the participatory brands like Rapha and Coachella, which mobilise movements of enthusiasts, participants, and fans.

2. The deadly serious game

"It's play that makes people unafraid to fail and confident to try new things. It's play that helps us do serious things better"

Jake Orlowitz, Wikipedia

Driving through Sydney with Sophie was a full-on experience. Sophie was clearly enjoying herself, but it was intense. First of all, there was the constant checking in with her fellow drivers about what was happening in other parts of the city. Then the constant checking of her dashboard-mounted phone to see how rates were fluctuating. There were the occasional whoops and curses when a customer posted a rating. And finally her obsession with breath mints—she was pretty certain the ones she had in the car were costing her rating points.

Like Google, WhatsApp, GoPro, and Spotify, Uber's primary purpose is the fulfilment of a social mission: "to make transportation as reliable as running water". Its mission is poetic, but also clear—Uber is out to make transportation as accessible and ubiquitous as possible.

Uber is a participatory business. It does not make cars, own cars, or hire them out. It enables others to participate. It connects people who want to travel, with the most efficient means to do so. It works on behalf of the user, not the seller.

What gives Uber its power, though, is that it's "gamified".

This is what kept Sophie stimulated and engaged, always on her toes. In the language of game theory, Uber is "coopetitive"—meaning it is both collaborative and competitive at the same time. There was a lot of camaraderie between the drivers Sophie connected with. They swapped ideas and tips. They alerted each other to where demand was rising. They worked together to reduce the saturation of cars in certain areas to help bring rates back up. They shared war stories, they made friends. But Sophie was also fiercely competitive. She wanted to top the rankings, improve her trip rates, and hit areas of peak demand before the others. The game for her was highly engaging but also deadly serious—her near-obsession with mints and how they might be affecting her rankings was just one tiny example of how significant and important the whole thing seemed to her.

So it wasn't just a game for Sophie—it was a "deadly serious game".

I saw the same behaviours that Sophie exhibited in the fast-growing tech start-ups I spent time in, and in the micro-companies and freelancers who were congregating in tech hubs. They were coopetitive at the level of the individual, but also at the level of the companies, too. There were meet-ups, gatherings, cross-industry groups. A tremendous movement of staff. People were networked by professional affiliation rather than the business they worked for. There was a huge sense of common purpose that created both a focus and a momentum. Results mattered a lot. Not just big end-of-project or end-of-year results, but the constant delivery from agile teams of apps, modules, experiments, and prototypes that could be tested and iterated.

And I saw it in the public sector, too. The London Borough of Newham is one of the poorest and most diverse neighbourhoods in the city, with a lot of social challenges. But a number of its state schools are punching way above their weight in terms of their pupils' success. When I visited high-performing state schools in London, other UK cities and in the United States, what I experienced was the deadly serious game! There was a coopetitive culture—highly collaborative and supportive yet with a great emphasis on individual achievement. This same coopetitive dynamic also existed between schools. What was noticeable was how each school was networked into communities, colleges, and mentoring schemes. There was a huge sense of common purpose, always led by passionate and motivated senior members of staff. Metrics and messaging were used to motivate rather than control.

I was surprised how stagnant and political many large aid agencies and corporate charities were: top-down hierarchies with an emphasis on procedure and position. But I saw the powerful dynamic of the deadly serious game operating in the thriving social enterprises I visited. Perhaps most charmingly, in a soap-making project I stumbled across in a remote Senegalese village, a tiny not-for-profit run by two American kids helping local women create micro-businesses. A few days earlier, I had been sitting on the harbour in Ziguinchor, a city that was once one of the centres of the world's slave trade (the town's name comes from the Portuguese for "I came and they cry") listening to a group of senior aid workers explain why enterprise didn't work in the region. But when I was with the soap-making project, I encountered a group of local women in a hot, run-down shed, determinedly learning both the technology and economics of making and selling soap using local materials. There was a beautiful camaraderie, and also an individual fierceness, as they worked on developing the means to help support and nurture both their families and their communities.

The cadence of the game was starkly different in different situations. It was a gentle dance in the recovery communities I visited in Australia and Asia. It was a dynamic flow in the yoga community in Bali where I did yoga teacher training. And an epic battle in the group of road cyclists whose support van I drove through the Alps and Pyrenees.

But the system was always the same. It was coopetitive. It was networked. It operated ground-up rather than top-down. And it played out as deadly serious to those involved.

The organisational model we have operated under for the past 200 years, and to some extent for the past 2,000, is the hierarchy. Democracies are hierarchies. Autocracies are hierarchies. Corporations are hierarchies. Traditional political parties are hierarchies. Pyramids where the power lies at the top and is applied top down. This model is now breaking down as rapidly proliferating digitally enabled networks erode their foundations.

The emergence of the deadly serious game as the organising model of high-performing organisations in the new paradigm points to two completely different possible futures.

There is a dystopian view, in which the game becomes a

mechanism for endless toil; where wealth is concentrated in the hands of rich hub and platforms owners; where organisations become mechanisms to drive down fees, maximise activity, and life becomes a frenzy of never-ending struggle; where there is always a next delivery; and where there's always someone after your job.

And there is a future we can design—where the game is the means to stimulate and support healthy, inclusive, connected societies, institutions, education, and work; where collaboration is kept in balance with competition; where the game is significant but not ferocious; and where its dynamic mechanism encourages contribution and personal growth, driving meritocracy and a fair distribution of wealth.

How it plays out is up to us.

The successful leaders in the emerging new paradigm will be those who have the capability to successfully leverage the mechanics of the game. But the shape, feel, and dynamic of our economies, lives, and societies will depend on the rules and metrics we choose to set.

The deadly serious game is the system that powers Apple's iTunes and App Store. It is the organising model of Facebook, Instagram and YouTube. It is the mechanism that creates the dynamic energy of Uber, Tindr, and Airbnb. It is the source of the explosive growth of participatory activities like yoga and road cycling.

Connected

1. Together

"We used to take belonging for granted. Cities used to be villages. Everyone knew each other, and everyone knew they had a place to call home. But after the mechanisation and Industrial Revolution of the last century, those feelings of trust and belonging were displaced by mass-produced and impersonal travel experiences. We also stopped trusting each other. And in doing so, we lost something essential about what it means to be a community. After all, our relationships with people will always be the most meaningful part of our lives"

Brian Chesky, CEO, Airbnb

The first thing Rachel Reis does when she arrives at the Green Note club in London's Camden Town is get everything out of the car. She then talks to the club's manager, then the sound man, then sets up her merchandising case near the door—she has recently created some handmade covers for a special limited edition of her new EP, so she arranges them carefully. Once she's got everything set up, she grabs a coffee and gets to work on her social media.

Rachel is from the Midwest of America and has only been in the UK for a few days. She has 15 gigs lined up in small venues across the country, then she's off to mainland Europe. This is on the back of a six-month tour of folk clubs and small venues across the States.

Ten years ago, Rachel might have expected her record label or her management to do all this. She might have left promotion to the venue or a local PR company. But then again, 10 years ago she probably would not have been able to do it at all.

Because 10 years ago, the music industry was operating as a hierarchy, a top-down pyramid that constrained and controlled access, restricting it to a chosen few. Today, it has become a giant networked game. The participation revolution has removed the barriers to access, like Uber, enabling an explosion of participation.

Some music industry executives and artists still mourn the passing of the era when people paid to passively consume their products, as if it was a golden age. But what the participation revolution has actually done is reconnect the music industry with its original social purpose. Rachel is a beautiful example of how this new movement works.

For the past few years, she had been performing as a solo artist, but this gig is the launch of her new band. Creating a band acknowledges what she is all about—collaboration, connection, doing things with others. It is a beautifully nuanced version of the coopetitive nature of the game. Rachel is an individual with a desire to achieve and succeed like any other artist, but she also does it deeply connected to and in collaboration with her community. She connects with other artists, with fans, with places to stay, and with venues. This requires a new attitude and relationship with fans. Rather than "Hey, I'm a rock star, come and watch me," it is more "Hey, here we are—let's do this together." There is an intimacy, empathy, and deep connectedness in how she works.

In the social economy, it is not that people won't spend money, it is about what they want to spend their money on. To succeed financially requires a shift of mindset from being on the side of the seller to siding with the user. Fans want unique experiences. They want to feel involved, they might want food and drink, they might want an artefact to take away. This requires deal making—between venues and artists, production staff, photographers. It becomes a collaborative venture. Rather than artists doing big deals with record labels that give them huge upfront development budgets but tie them into restrictive long-term contracts, this new economy is about building social ecosystems that are self-sustaining. Rachel has patrons: loyal fans who provide money to help her develop new work.

But she isn't in the business of selling music, albums, or merchandising, although these all certainly contribute to a portfolio of ways to generate funds. Her gigs aren't really about the music, beautiful as it is.

In a world where music can be heard, listened to and streamed from anywhere, anytime, it has become a commodity. The value of what Rachel does isn't in the tunes. It is something you only really understand by being there.

In 2008, Adam Neumann and Miguel McKelvey set up GreenDesk, a co-working space in a rapidly gentrifying neighbourhood in Brooklyn, New York.

GreenDesk was designed as an eco-friendly, collaborative, and highly communal work space for an emerging community of freelance designers and geeks, who would soon become known as hipsters.

Neumann and McKelvey had noticed that increasing numbers of young people were either freelancing or starting up small enterprises. They were an interesting lot. On the one hand, they were fiercely independent, while on the other, they were collaborative and social; they thrived on sharing their thoughts and ideas.

GreenDesk therefore worked on two levels: it offered pay-as-you-go desk space, with fast Internet access, good lighting, and a physical environmental as green and nice as it could be, but it also had a strong focus on community. There were communal spaces, a café with healthy food, places to hang out. People were encouraged to put on events, share what they did. None of it was mandated—there was no cheer squad or corporate HR—it was simply encouraged and empowered. GreenDesk exuded the philosophy of a garden; an environment in which a community could organically grow, rather than something that was engineered.

There was a vibe at GreenDesk, and you could feel it as soon as you walked in. It was a highly productive environment—a lot of work got done. But when people weren't working, or just as part of their creative process, they connected and hung out. It was the same invisible energy that courses through Homeboy—fierce and nurturing at the same time.

In 2010, Neumann and McKelvey sold GreenDesk and decided to take what they had learned and implement it on a larger scale.

They called their new business "WeWork".

When businesses rapidly scale, they often lose the essence of what first made them special. They become something to franchise or "roll out". But Neumann and McKelvey were keenly aware of what it was that had made GreenDesk so special. It wasn't the shared office space, although that was vital. It was the fellowship, the intimacy, the sense of belonging, camaraderie, and shared experience.

They made this special quality WeWork's primary focus, its social mission: to create a world where people work to create a life, not just a living.

I covered a lot of ground researching this book. I travelled through every continent except Antarctica (and I apologise if I missed some good stuff going on down there). I visited high-tech businesses and low-tech businesses, for-profits and not-for-profits, oil companies, addiction clinics, and NGOs. I hung out in tech hubs, hackathons, coffee shops, and yoga festivals. I lived for periods in Europe, North America, Australia, and Asia.

And as I travelled, I started to see the patterns. I started to see how a new kind of enterprise was emerging. I started to see how they thought differently, operated differently, and organised themselves differently.

But most crucially, I realised that what really made them different was how they *felt*.

Once I had seen this, I went looking for it, and wherever I found it I saw what a difference it made.

That invisible thing that we all know when we feel it, but can't ever truly put our finger on.

Carlo named it as we watched the sun go down in Echo Park.

Connection.

It pulsed through the high-growth tech companies that are really changing the way the world works, the open-source projects, the gaming communities, the social innovators. It flowed through the wellbeing movements like road cycling and yoga. It danced around the edges of the corporations that are really pulling out all the stops to transform, like wisps of mist in the morning.

When I visited villages like Acciaroli in Italy and Ikaria in Greece—places known to have far higher than average levels of wellbeing and longevity—it was tangible, in the streets, in the cafés where people of all ages hung out and talked.

It glowed in the addiction recovery communities I visited, the code club in a prison where groups of inmates developed skills together for when they got out, the inner-city schools I went to that are performing way above the odds.

It is what makes Rachel Reis's gigs so beguiling. They offer fellowship, intimacy, a shared collective experience. There's a beauty to the songs, a delight in the craft and skills of the musicians. But what they are really about is connection—authentic, real, deep, human connection.

Everywhere that I experienced thriving, growing organisations, I felt it, and everywhere that I experienced stagnation or lack of growth, it was notably missing. There might have been a vision, and change initiatives, new office fit-outs, diversity programs, and employee perks. But that *thing*, that feeling of connection—it just wasn't there.

We are living in increasingly socially dislocated times. There are more than 33,000 gangs in the United States, similar to the one that Carlo was a member of. At any one time, more than 1.5 million gang members are actively involved in crime.

Depression and mental health issues are on the rise.

In the US, more than 12 million people regularly abuse opiates. The prescription opiate Oxycontin has become so widely misused, it is known in some places as "hillbilly heroin". Each year, more than 40,000 people are admitted to emergency rooms, having either overdosed on it or had a mental breakdown.

In 2016, research released by the National Health Service in the UK showed that one in four women between the ages of 16 and 24 regularly self-harm. A similar number have eating disorders, hyper-anxiety, and depression. One in eight exhibit the symptoms of profound post-traumatic stress disorder.

In Western countries, divorce rates have spiralled upwards. Some 42 percent of first marriages fail in the UK and 53 percent split up in America, with rates as high as 71 percent in Belgium. Rates of divorce in second marriages are much higher. More and more people are living alone. Research published in 2015 shows that people who become socially isolated for protracted periods are nearly 40 percent more likely to die early.

In a world that is fragmenting, changing, breaking down, connection—authentic, real, tangible, human, emotional, spiritual, whatever you want to call it, connection—is the thing we all seek most, and the thing we all need most.

Consumerism has hollowed out our societies. It has left us wanting, needing, and, in many cases, craving something far deeper than just more "stuff".

This is a "sun is the centre of the universe" insight. Perhaps *the* "sun is the centre of the universe" insight.

Human connection is the currency of the social economy. It is potentially the most abundant and sustainable energy source on the planet, yet for so many it is the scarcest.

By the end of 2016, WeWork had 80,000 members in 110 locations all around world.

In February 2017, the business was valued at $20 billion.

2 Ours

"I know that may sound strange to some people, but most important is my connection with my fans and the connection that they breed with one another"

Lady Gaga

In May 2012, word began to spread that the British indie band the Stone Roses were going to play a free gig at Warrington Town Hall, a small and decidedly unglamorous venue in the hometown of lead singer Ian Brown. It would be the first time the band had played together in more than 15 years.

The venue held 1,000 people, and to get a ticket you'd have to prove you were a fan—that meant turning up with a piece of memorabilia or an original vinyl album. Tickets were not going to be available online; you'd have to go to the town hall to get one.

Word spread via social networks and local radio. The tickets were snapped up in a matter of hours, with hundreds of would-be concert-goers left disappointed.

The gig was a huge success. Word got out, pictures went onto social media. It wasn't just that the Stone Roses were back, it was that the vibe was back; that sense of connection.

More gigs followed. When the band had played together 15 years earlier, it was as part of massive tour to promote an album. This time, though, there was no album, no "product"—just gigs. Instead of employing a big-bang top-down marketing campaign, the band focused their attention on their fans.

On 27 September 2016, Donald Trump stepped onstage in front of a massive crowd of 15,000 people in Melbourne, Florida. Outside, another 10,000 Trump fans were clamouring to get in. About 650 miles north in Raleigh, North Carolina, his rival Hillary Clinton was addressing 1,400 supporters at Wake Tech Community College.

There was a little over a month to go in the American presidential election, and Trump was well behind in the polls. Every expert, every opinion poll—even the ones that often went against the grain—said he had practically no chance of winning.

Despite the majority of the mainstream media, and just about every high-profile political pundit and establishment figure going, being vehemently against Trump, something was happening on the ground.

The Stone Roses and Donald Trump employed the same strategy as the high-growth social businesses like Facebook, WhatsApp, and Instagram. Instead of using traditional top-down methods of marketing and engagement, they worked from the bottom up. They focused their attention on their fans.

The successful businesses and enterprises in the emerging new paradigm don't have customers, they have fans. And fans have an entirely different relationship with the things they care about and love.

On 8 November 2016, Donald Trump won the American presidential election, defying every mainstream poll. Much was said in the aftermath about Trump's many controversial views, including his seemingly backward ideas about energy policy and climate change. In the weeks after his win, though, the biggest threat to the polar ice cap was probably from server farms overheating as social media went ballistic.

The seeds of Trump's success were planted in places like Melbourne, Florida. He focused his attention on empowering fans. He enabled participation. He built a movement from the ground up, and in so doing, triggered a "social retrovirus"—a network of fans that, once constructed, has an explosive energy of its own, a growth pattern that defies traditional analytics and measurement. The Democratic Party had won Florida in the two previous general elections. And several years before that, in 2000, in a highly contested result, George Bush captured the state for the Republican Party by a mere 500 votes. In 2016, Trump won Florida by more than 100,000 votes.

This is the dynamics of the new paradigm. Networked rather than hierarchical. Participatory. Movements of fans built from the bottom up.

Six months after the Stone Roses played their first gig in 15 years in Warrington Town Hall, tickets were released for two gigs at Heaton Park in Manchester—an outdoor venue that held 70,000 people. The tickets sold out in just 14 minutes. It would have been much quicker if the ticketing websites hadn't been so overwhelmed. A third gig was quickly added, selling out in under an hour. In a total of 68 minutes, the band sold more than 220,000 tickets, netting £11 million in revenue, making the three nights the fastest-selling gigs in UK history.

Strategic shifts

Consumer economics	Social economics
What	Why
Products	Participation
Them	Us

The process of transformation

"Too often we let our thinking and our beliefs about what we 'know' prevent us from seeing things as they really are. We tend to take the ordinary for granted and fail to grasp the extraordinariness of the ordinary. To see the richness of the present moment, we need to cultivate what has been called 'beginner's mind', a mind that is willing to see everything as if for the first time.

"An open, 'beginner's mind' allows us to be receptive to new possibilities and prevents us from getting stuck in the rut of our own expertise, which often thinks it knows more than it does"

Jon Kabat-Zinn, *Full Catastrophe Living*

There is an old Buddhist tale that goes something like this: a group of monks are on the path to enlightenment. They have been working with Buddha for many years, doing everything he asks. It's tough, as he is continually challenging them to let go of their old ideas.

Eventually they become frustrated.

"Lord Buddha," they say, trying to hide their impatience.

Introduction

"You promised us enlightenment. We know these things take time, but really. We've done everything you asked. Please, we need to know—when will we be enlightened?"

"Enlightenment comes as you seek Nirvana," Buddha replies, with an encouraging smile. "You will know when it has happened." Now the monks have heard Buddha speak like this many times before. What had once seemed profound and spiritual—and a great means to impress people at parties—was beginning to sound decidedly like New Age claptrap to them.

"Look, we can't keep going like this," they say. "We need some clarity, give us the skinny version."

"OK," Buddha sighs, when it becomes clear they are not going to stand down.

He ushers them over to the window.

"See that mountain over there?" he says, pointing at a golden peak far away on the horizon. "That is Nirvana. When you get there you will be enlightened."

The monks gaze at the mountain for a moment, their faces soft and smiling.

"And how do we get there?" they ask.

Buddha points to the dense forest that lies between where they are and the mountain.

"Through there."

"But that is twice as dark and thick as the one we just came through," the monks say with alarm. "We have no idea how to get through there."

"Exactly," says Buddha. "See you on the other side!"

ARCHITECTURE

1. Create a cause

- **Make your primary purpose the fulfilment of a social mission**
  Why over what
  On the side of the user
  Singularity of purpose

- **Take a stand**
  Worthwhile and meaningful
  Out to prove a point

- **Innovate on the field of play**
  Demand side
  Whole human experience
  Participatory innovation

2. Mobilise a movement

- **Enable participation**
  Participation over content
  Tools over products

- **Make it a game—a deadly serious game**
  Coopetitive
  Significant
  Networked

3. Build a community

- **Facilitate fellowship**
  Belonging
  Intimacy
  Shared experience

- **Empower fans**
  Identification
  Affiliation
  Ownership

II. Case stories

1. We are United!

"I fell in love with football as I was later to fall in love with women: suddenly, inexplicably, uncritically, giving no thought to the pain or disruption it would bring with it"

Nick Hornby, *Fever Pitch*

There's a moment when a peaceful protest can suddenly erupt into something dangerous and violent, and it feels like we are getting pretty close to it.

"Back off," a voice urges through a loud hailer as the police cordon starts to push forward. *"Back! Off!"*

Somewhere behind us a smoke bomb has gone off. Plumes of acrid smog billow into the overcast sky, infusing it with a blood-red tinge. It matches the mood. There is an ugly, menacing energy pulsing through the crowd.

I look around. Men, who, a few minutes ago, were happily chanting protests, some even laughing, are now screaming insults and death threats.

In a world increasingly fraught with conflict and turmoil, we could be in many places—any one of dozens of political flashpoints across the globe. We could be protesting against austerity in Europe, against globalisation wherever the WTO is meeting, or against the government just about anywhere.

But as far as those around me are concerned, we are here to protest against something far more important than that.

We are outside a sporting arena in Manchester, in the north of England. More specifically, we are outside Old Trafford, the home of Manchester United, the most valuable and most supported sports club on the planet.

United are about to play AC Milan in the European Champions League. It is a high-profile game and the city is flooded with fans from across the globe. Many are doing what fans do when they travel: drinking, singing, and having fun.

A large group, though, has come to the ground early to mount a protest. United's fans have been unhappy with the club's American owners, the Glazers, ever since they bought the club in a highly leveraged buyout. They are angry at the huge debt the family took on to buy the club, worried about their track record with the other professional sporting franchise they own, (American football's Tampa Bay Buccaneers) and generally of the opinion that they have no understanding of, or interest in, the traditions or history of English football. Over the past couple of seasons, momentum has been building.

Today, things seem to have come to a head. The number of fans outside the ground is unprecedented. Their anger and frustration have reached boiling point. The Champions League pulls in a massive global TV audience, and the fans clearly want the whole world to see what is happening at United.

When the game kicks off, tens of millions of TV viewers around the globe are met with an extraordinary sight. United are famous for their bright red colours— earning the club its nickname, "the Red Devils"—but as the whistle blows, fans in every section of the ground unfurl green and gold flags, almost blotting out the official red. It as an act of defiance, as well as a nod to history—green and gold are the colours of "Newton Heath," the club that Manchester United grew out of when the game was still amateur. The colours are the result of a grassroots movement by fans, keen to show who really owns the club. It looks as if there are as many fans in the ground wearing green and gold shirts as there are wearing red; since an unofficial green and gold shirt went on sale, more than 30,000 have been sold.

As the match progresses, and United take a three-nil lead, protests and angry anti-Glazer chants rage on. When Darren Fletcher seals the game for United with a fourth goal, the fans barely break their protest to cheer. At the final whistle, green and gold scarves rain down on the pitch, and a massive banner is unfurled from a balcony in one of the central stands—"United Against the Glazers" it reads. The atmosphere and energy in the ground is explosive.

Just as it seem like things can't get any worse for the Glazers, they do. David Beckham, United's erstwhile pin-up boy, and now a pin-up boy for the whole world, has been playing for Milan. This is his first time playing back at the ground where he made his name.

Beckham has been jogging around the side of the ground, acknowledging United's fans in an act of mutual admiration. As he reaches the Stretford End, home of Old Trafford's most fervent supporters, he stoops down and scoops up a discarded green and gold scarf and wraps it around his neck. The fans go wild. This is a significant gesture from a politically careful man. Beckham is with them.

The TV cameras race to pick out the Glazers on the VIP balcony, keen to see their reaction.

And this is when something even more surprising than Beckham picking up the scarf happens.

You might expect a group of people who'd taken on half

a billion dollars of debt to buy a football club, only to see the team's supporters turn violently against them, to look pretty worried.

But as the camera pans across the face of Joel Glazer, the club's president—as he looks out at the banners, at the fans, at Beckham, and no doubt is able to hear some of the awful personal insults being hurled at him—he smiles. It is only fleeting, but noticeable. Not only does he smile, but he smiles in a way that suggests he is really quite happy.

Caught up in the drama of the fans' story, it is extremely difficult to understand what on earth he could have to smile about.

But understanding what that smile is about lies at the heart of understanding not only why sports franchises like Manchester United are so successful, but what makes many of the disruptive new businesses and movements that are emerging in the 21st century so successful.

If you listen to the fans, and the barrage of stories in the news, it seems like the Glazers have their backs up against the wall, that everyone is against them, that they have no choice but to go. The media has been stoking the fire so hard, you'd expect Glazer to look terrified, or perhaps even be out the back clearing his desk.

And if you apply conventional business wisdom to the situation, then it looks like the club is experiencing a PR disaster; you don't need an MBA to know that customers threatening to kill your CEO is a sign they are not very happy. If you adhere to the old maxim "The customer is king," then it looks like Joel Glazer is doing a terrible job indeed.

But if you look from the point of view of Glazer himself, you see something entirely different. What Glazer sees is one of the largest football grounds in the UK packed to capacity with people who have paid a lot of money to get in (and for every person in the ground, there are 10 more clamouring for tickets). Sure, they are yelling and shouting and baying for his blood, but the critical issue is that they are doing so inside not outside the ground, having paid handsomely for the privilege. What is more, they have been doing it week after week. What he sees is a business that can depend on its fans to keep turning up, and to keep spending a lot of money, whatever they feel about him or the club. Much as the 30,000 alternative green and gold shirts represent lost sales, it is a drop in the ocean compared with the two million official red United shirts that have been sold worldwide throughout the season—an increase from the year before that far exceeds the number of green and gold shirts sold. What is more, United are through to the next round of the Champions League, an incredibly lucrative competition. If this is a bad day at the office, imagine what a good one would look like. No wonder Glazer is smiling.

A few months after the Champions League game, United's brand is valued at $412 million, an increase of 10 percent on the previous year. This figure makes Manchester United the most valuable sporting franchise in the world. It is given a AAA credit rating—this is in the heart of the global financial crisis when all around, previously rock-solid businesses, and even countries, are losing theirs.

Two years year later, Forbes Magazine values the club at $3 billion, a billion more than any other sporting franchise—and a sixfold increase in 24 months. In the same year, market research company Cantor estimates that the club has 659 million fans worldwide, more than half of them in Asia. To give that number some context, it would mean one in 10 of the world's population supports United. Other research organisations dispute the figure, and a more conservative estimate of 300 million is suggested: that's a mere one in 18 of the world's population, or the equivalent of the total population of the United States.

If fans were normal customers, Manchester United would have had a disaster on its hands—sales would have plummeted, customers would have left, board members would have been fired. But they are not normal customers, and as the figures showed, the business actually got much stronger. To a fan, paying a lot of money to enter the ground week after week to let your feelings be known is a perfectly logical thing to do. For anyone else, it would be insane, like continually going to a grocery store and buying expensive food you don't like and complaining bitterly about it at the checkout counter.

A few years later, I am sitting behind a one-way mirror watching some consumer research. It is being conducted by a small specialist company with a reputation for being able to tease out deep insight into consumer behaviour. What the study is interested in finding out is why people switch from one mobile phone brand to another—or, more specifically, what it is that stops them. The study is focused on high-earning women.

In the room is a 37-year-old woman named Jay, who is on her third generation of iPhone. Jay is a confident, highly intelligent woman. She is a successful lawyer, so she is both analytical and used to making decisions. She is clearly quite bemused to be there.

Jay has been chosen as she reported being particularly disgruntled with her current phone and is thinking of replacing it. There's a new iPhone in the pipeline as well as a whole host of new handsets from competitors. The interviewer is interested in what will drive her decision to switch.

As the interview starts to unfold, the interviewer explores what it is Jay doesn't like about her current phone. She then looks at whether the new iPhone coming out will solve all Jay's problems, and it is clear it won't; Jay is a bright woman—she has done her research. The interviewer then starts to steer Jay toward a new Samsung model, as it seems not only to give her the functionality and features she currently has plus the new ones she wants, but also to be less expensive.

But as the interviewer highlights each benefit, Jay kicks back against them. She seems intent on proving the interviewer wrong, citing anecdotal examples or just vague fears why she thinks the Samsung might be a bad idea. But the interviewer has a strong case, and eventually—and quite reluctantly—Jay comes around. She is, after all, a logical consumer. The Samsung does everything she wants, she admits it is well designed, it has a bigger screen, better battery life, and it's cheaper.

It is clearly the winning proposition.

The interviewer then asks Jay if she will therefore buy a Samsung. There is a long gap, and a lot of umming and ahing.

"No," Jay eventually says, a little embarrassed.

"Why not?" the interviewer asks.

Jay pauses. "I don't know…it's… I dunno, I am just not sure if I am ready to let go of my Apple."

The interviewer then asks if Jay would take the Samsung if it were free. Jay hesitates. It looks for a moment like she is going to say no, then her faces lightens. "Yes," she says, laughing.

"Why so?" the interviewer asks.

"Because I could then sell it on eBay and use the money toward a new iPhone." She is smiling, clearly aware of the incongruity of what she is saying.

Jay is bright and self-aware, but she clearly has no idea why she is so attached to her iPhone. Even though she is disgruntled with it and a far better alternative seems to be available, she can't bring herself to switch. You can see the lawyer in her battle with that.

If you look at Jay as a customer, her behaviour doesn't make sense. We live in incredibly impatient and intolerant times. Consumers' expectations have gone through the roof while their tolerance levels have tanked. Ask anyone who works in a call centre what it is like to deal with customers and you will hear some pretty grim tales. Trust and loyalty have hit an all-time low. Bright, savvy customers like Jay know how to get a good deal. If she were thinking and acting like a normal customer, Apple would be toast.

But she isn't. Jay's behaviour mirrors that of the Manchester United supporters on the terraces at Old Trafford. Jay isn't an Apple customer, she is an Apple fan—which means she has a totally different relationship with the brand. This is what Apple—and particularly Steve Jobs, when he was at the helm—has known for years, and what Nokia totally missed when they opened their concept store.

Apple doesn't have customers, it has fans. And you don't get fans simply by opening a flashy store.

If you look at the relationship governments, political parties, and many other public service organisations now have with those they allegedly serve, you see the same increasingly acrimonious relationship as conventional businesses are having with customers. Their mistake was to start to think of them as customers.

But while customer satisfaction is tending to zero, and governments and institutions around the world are in what looks like a full-scale war with many of those they are meant to serve, fan loyalty is sky-rocketing. Apple fans like Jay who find their current model doesn't do what they want, simply trade up—a poor battery life isn't a reason to look elsewhere, it is an opportunity for a new model. Many will wait patiently for a long time until the next Apple model comes out rather than going elsewhere. In fact, the waiting is part of the fun. Fans help each other out and act as far more effective salespeople than a good-looking assistant in a store. Kids don't think they are being "upsold" when their parents take them to their first football game—it's the same when a fellow Apple fan gives you a heads-up on a new app. Product launches have become quasi-religious events that make the front page of newspapers, providing zero-cost advertising, a CMO's dream. Like Manchester United's value, Apple's stock and market capitalisation has gone through the roof.

The successful businesses and enterprises in the emerging new paradigm don't have customers, they have fans. And fans have a very different relationship with the things they care about and love.

This is why Joel Glazer was smiling. Fans, however unhappy they might be, are really good for business; customers are really not.

In January 2017, after four years of chronic underperformance, management turmoil and mass fan outrage, the accountancy company Deloitte announced that Manchester United generated £515 million revenue during the 2015–2016 season, a whopping 33 percent increase on the previous year—placing it firmly on top of the list of most valuable sports clubs. In the same period, the average productivity of corporations fell by 0.6 percent, consistent with a trend that has seen productivity flatline for more than a decade.

2. The power of fans

"I live my life completely serving only my work and my fans. My fans have cultivated my talent and they continue to nurture me"

Lady Gaga

On 16 January 2006, a song titled "I Bet You Look Good on the Dancefloor" by the British band Arctic Monkeys entered the UK singles chart at number one. Going straight in at number one is highly unusual, but not unheard of for some very big acts. Arctic Monkeys were not a big act, though. In fact, very few people had ever heard of them. They were an indie outfit from the north of England with a retro punk style that was totally out of step with the other music making the charts at the time. The song was also their first single, and released on a small indie label. It had not been pushed by any big advertising or marketing campaign. Going straight in at number one for any band was a big deal. But for the debut single of an indie band with no big record company backing, it was unprecedented. The most common response to people hearing about the band was, "Arctic who?"

The astonishing success of Arctic Monkeys, both then and since, is testament not just to the power of fans, but to a particular kind of relationship between fans and the entity they support; one that the band maintains to this day.

Arctic Monkeys were formed in Sheffield in 2003 and started gigging in small clubs and pubs around the city. Their style was unashamedly indie, with an honesty and vigour that connected well with Sheffield's notoriously purist indie scene. They soon attracted a loyal and passionate local following and started to look around for a studio to record some demo tracks. Their motivation wasn't to record a single or cut an album to sell, though. What they were interested in was recording some tracks to give away when they played, so their fans could hear their songs better, as their gigs were raucous. They found a studio housed in a slightly dilapidated old cutlery factory, one of the many buildings that had fallen into disrepair after the demise of the city's steel industry, and recorded 17 tracks.

"We never made those demos to make money or anything," the band's drummer, Matt Helders, said in an interview soon after the first single broke. "We were giving them away free anyway—that was a better way for people to hear them."

Since the band was giving the tracks away, fans knew it was OK to share them with others, and began to file-share them on the Internet. One of the first fans to share them online put the tracks in a folder named "Boardwalk," as he'd been given the CD at a gig in the Boardwalk Hotel, an influential venue in Sheffield's indie music scene. When the band later decided to retrofit a title to the collection, they called it Beneath the Boardwalk, a nod to this source, and a testament to the fans' close involvement with the band's development.

This was all happening at a time when the mainstream music industry was dragging fans into the courts and suing them for file-sharing, making cult bands like Metallica suddenly look decidedly corporate.

Arctic Monkeys' music began to spread. Unbeknown to the band, a group of fans set up a MySpace site, sharing news, pictures and the demo tracks, and a local filmmaker, caught up in the infectious DIY and "open-source" ethos surrounding the band, started filming their gigs and releasing them on his own website under the title "Fake Tales of San Francisco".

The band's music and reputation began to spread peer-to-peer. There was no "them and us" hierarchy, no big record company broadcasting down from on high. It was a flat structure, spreading out rather than down. The band released a single on their own label, making just 500 CDs and 1,000 seven-inch vinyl records, and also releasing the track as an MP3 on iTunes. The CDs and vinyl sold out fast, and people began to buy the tracks online. The indie music press started to notice the phenomenon. This led to the band being given a slot on a small stage reserved for little-known and unsigned bands at the Reading and Leeds Festivals.

When the band played at Reading, so many people turned up the stage was overwhelmed. The same happened again at Leeds, leaving the event organisers perplexed: where had all the fans come from?

Momentum was building. The fan-run MySpace site covered the festival gigs. Now new fans started sharing the music.

The band members were keen to work with enthusiasts with an empathy for their music, so they decided to sign with a small indie label called Domino, run out of the front room of a house in Leeds, rather than with a big major.

No one expected what happened next. When "I Bet You Look Good on the Dancefloor" was released, it sold out in days, barrelling straight into the UK singles charts at number one, beating Robbie Williams, a global phenomenon, whose new release had massive advertising and promotional backing. The band's second single, released a couple of months later, also went straight in at number one.

When Arctic Monkeys released their debut album, *Whatever People Say I Am, That's What I'm Not*—not exactly the catchiest of titles—it became the fastest-selling debut album in British music history, quickly going platinum.

Since then, the band has stayed true to their fans and indie roots, releasing five albums, each with a very different tone from the last—flying in the face of music industry "best practice", which says once something has been successful with a certain sound, you stick with it. They make music they love, and share it with the people they know will also love it, as it's been tested out on the road, in pubs and clubs, among fans with whom they have a deep connection and empathy.

Arctic Monkeys are not four men from Sheffield who play music. They are a huge community of fans, who all share their love and passion for the music with one another. Because every fan is free to contribute and take part, information and ideas spread out fan-to-fan rather than from some central hub. This creates a self-generating and ever-expanding network, in which every node is active. This network effect gives it the ability to grow and spread with a dynamic similar to that of a biological virus.

What makes the viral nature of networks of fans so virulent is their fidelity. Fans don't just randomly pass stuff on. They are discerning, thoughtful and caring. They trust those they receive from and direct to other like-minded people. This creates a high likelihood that recipients will not only share what they receive, but share it with vigour and passion—passing it on like a gift. The result is that the network proliferates rapidly, as every individual actively engages others. This explosive action is how Arctic Monkeys were able to come seemingly from nowhere, completely blindsiding the music industry.

What makes networks of fans really potent, though, is that not only are they virulent, they are also highly resilient. Conventional viruses tend to diminish just as quickly as they emerge, the network collapsing rapidly once the initial heat burns off. Biological viruses like flu strains flare up and scare the living daylights out of us all, then disappear. Social viruses in the form of fashions and fads come and go in the same way.

But networks of fans don't just stay in place, they actually get stronger. The reason for this is that their action isn't simply viral. It is "retroviral"—it actually changes the nature of those with whom it comes in contact. In biology, a retrovirus doesn't just infect the cells of its recipient, it gets right inside the DNA, permanently changing its makeup. Social retroviruses do the same—they don't just pass from peer to peer, they get inside the hearts and minds of their recipients, permanently changing their attitudes and behaviour. Fans beget fans.

The retroviral nature of networks of fans is what enabled Arctic Monkeys not only to blindside the music industry, but also to get stronger once they got there. As we saw with Manchester United, fans are extremely loyal, tenacious, and committed to the cause. Managers, owners, players, band members and customers, in particular—all come and go. But fans don't.

Arctic Monkeys have won five BRIT Awards, including two for Best British Group, and have twice been nominated for Grammy Awards. *Whatever People Say I Am, That's What I'm Not* won the Mercury Prize for best album, and is listed in Rolling Stone magazine's top 500 albums of all time. It still remains the fastest-selling debut album by any group in the UK.

In June 2013, the band headlined at the Glastonbury Festival, playing to 100,000 fans. The surge for tickets when they were released brought the festival's website to a standstill.

3. How to be a billionaire in three easy moves: part 1

"Every start-up should address a real and demonstrated need in the world—if you build a solution to a problem lots of people have, it's so easy to sell your product to the world"

Kevin Systrom, co-founder, Instagram

Putri gesticulates to her friends to move a little to the left. She is determined to frame them between two of the big stone bells that make up the perimeter of the temple. The sun is starting to set, and for the first time all day there is good light.

"Quick," she says, waving her hand. She takes a picture, checks it, and grimaces—however hard she tries, a Chinese family keeps wandering into view. She is determined to capture a clear view of the mountains that rise above the rice fields in the background.

"Again!" she shouts, and her friends retake their position, giggling and making V peace signs with their fingers.

Eventually, she is happy. Her friends cluster around her to take a look at their picture.

The women are all from Indonesia, but speak mainly in

English. They work for Garuda, Indonesia's national airline, and are keen to get rostered on long-haul international flights, so they practise whenever they can. Because English is also the *lingua franca* of most of the music, movies, and social media they like, even when they are not consciously practising, they fall in and out of it; their sentences switching between their native Bahasa and a heavily accented but fluent American English.

Putri tries out a couple of filters. When everyone is in agreement, she posts the image.

There is something magical about the Borobudur temple. It is the largest Buddhist temple in the world. It rises up in the middle of a tropical basin like an Indonesian Camelot, the steam from the palm-studded rice fields shrouding it in mist. The route to the top is a long spiral, passing 504 statues of Buddha, each housed in an ornately carved stone structure that looks like a bell. The climb signifies the path to Nirvana.

When the women reach the summit, they stop to take in the view and cool down. Putri checks her Instagram app. She has 23 likes for the picture and 12 comments. She smiles and types a reply.

"That creepy Dutch guy says you look hot," she says to Ita, and they all laugh.

"*Ih enggak banget*," (no way!) Ita says, feigning a shudder.

Putri lies down on the stone bench while her friends go off to look at the view. She points her phone at herself, tosses her hair, and moves her face to catch the late afternoon sunlight. Then she posts a picture.

Instagram was first released as a free app for the iPhone in October 2010. Like Arctic Monkeys' debut single, it wasn't launched by a big industry player, but came out of a small independent studio in San Francisco, developed by a tight-knit group of designers and programmers who initially worked part-time. The app was passed on in the same way as Arctic Monkeys' early demo tracks—shared among the development team's network of fellow enthusiasts, who used it to make images and share them with their friends, who then repeated the process. People loved it. Within just a few months, it had hundreds of thousands of users.

It was an impressive surge, but a combination of easy access, no cost, and novelty meant that many apps initially spread rapidly, only to fall out of favour when the next shiny new thing emerged.

What kicked Instagram beyond fad, though, was when its developers added the ability to tag images in early 2011. This was when the retroviral network effect kicked in.

Biological retroviruses are malignant in nature—HIV being the highest-profile example. They negatively affect their recipients, often severely compromising them. But social retroviruses spread because they are altruistic—they positively change the lives of their hosts. Hashtags meant that users could connect and build relationships based around shared interests.

Instagram started to weave its way into the social fabric of its users' lives as communities emerged and relationships were formed that didn't exist anywhere else. Putri initially intended to use it to share with her friends and family in Jakarta, but very quickly started to connect with flight crews and others she had never met around the world. She now can't imagine travelling without it. When I ask her what her life would be like if she weren't allowed to use Instagram, she shudders: "Lonely," is her first response.

Once the retroviral effect was in play, the app became highly contagious. Less than nine months after the addition of hashtags, Instagram's active user base hit 10 million. From there, it kept snowballing, showing the same kind of explosive growth that so wrong-footed the promoters at the first festivals that Arctic Monkeys played at—droves of fans just seemed to appear out of nowhere.

On 3 April 2012, Instagram released a version of the app for the Android operating system, opening it up for the first time to non-iPhone users. On that first day alone, more than a million copies were downloaded, pushing its overall user base to over 30 million.

Just seven days after the Android release, Mark Zuckerberg, CEO of Facebook, announced that his company was buying Instagram for $1 billion in cash and stock, rocketing Kevin Systrom and Mike Krieger, Instagram's two twenty-something founders, into the super-rich list overnight.

Start-up to billion-dollar buyout in under two years—it was a dizzying tale of success.

Both Arctic Monkeys' and Instagram's astonishing rise to prominence are testament to the power of fans and the retroviral effect. Together, they explain how an indie band from Sheffield with no backing and an app from a tiny studio in San Francisco were able to grow so quickly and become so dominant.

What they don't explain, though, is why they succeeded while others didn't.

Instagram wasn't the first photo-processing app. It wasn't the first to provide the ability to share with others. And in terms of functionality and features, it was far from the best; its pictures were low resolution and didn't allow zooming— you could tap and swipe as much as you liked and its images remained stubbornly small.

Fans trust each other, which is why they are open to what is shared with them. And they are generous, which is why they so readily share with others. But they are also incredibly discerning. If there isn't something very special about what comes their way, they won't pass it on. Reputation is really important to a fan.

San Francisco's hipsters, like Sheffield's indie music fans, are notoriously picky. They had access to some of the newest and best technology available, including a whole host of state-of-the-art photo processing packages, many much more sophisticated than Instagram.

From a functionality point of view, it isn't immediately obvious why fans were so enamoured with it.

But then in terms of pure functional design, Nokia should have been able to beat Apple hands down when it launched the iPhone, but it didn't—with devastating consequences for the company.

And an intelligent consumer like Jay should clearly have gone with a Samsung phone, but she didn't.

The reason fans took to Instagram was about something far more fundamental than clever tech.

While the app was developed in San Francisco, the source of its success wasn't a high-tech design studio in the city's Mission District or a hipster café in SoMa. In fact, it wasn't even in the city.

It can be traced back to a decidedly unhip small town way over on the other side of the country in upstate New York. More specifically, to the bedroom of a twenty-something man who still lived with his mum.

He had all the hallmarks of a geek: part hipster, part nerd, socially gregarious and awkward in equal measure. He loved music and travel and, like Arctic Monkeys, was connected into a community of like-minded souls.

When he was 24 years old, he decided to take a trip to the Dominican Republic. He'd been enchanted by pictures he'd seen of its capital city, Santo Domingo, and was excited to go there. He was also keen to share some of his experiences with his friends and family, so he asked a friend who was into photography for advice on the best equipment to take. His friend recommended some expensive state-of-the-art gear, which he duly bought.

When he arrived in Santo Domingo, he was immediately disappointed with his purchase. The city's cobbled streets throbbed with life and he found that the camera equipment got in the way. It was bulky and needed to be lugged around. It was also complicated. He wanted to move swiftly and capture critical moments. By the time he'd set up the camera, the moment was usually lost. He quickly stopped using it.

On the journey back home, he started to think about the camera—it was nagging at him. Rather than improve his holiday, the photography equipment had actually disrupted it; the exact opposite of what he had hoped for. He started to wonder what might have made his experience better.

When he got home, he went to work, hacking together a prototype with a small group of fellow geeks. It was a lean, agile process, with its focus on solving the problem he had experienced on holiday.

He knew from his own foray into photography that what they developed must enhance the experience rather than get in the way. He knew that capturing the feel of a moment was far more important than accuracy. He wasn't interested in apertures and lenses and loading film, he'd just wanted to point and shoot. He understood from his own experience what was important, and the team didn't cease until what they had come up with achieved that aim.

They created a beta version and shared it with their fellow enthusiasts.

Within just a couple of months, the early version was being

snapped up by fellow enthusiasts, who loved the simplicity and ease with which they could capture and share moments of their lives with their friends, who then, in turn, wanted to join in. Just as with Arctic Monkeys, a retroviral network of fans began to build.

It was an innovation that made the young man fantastically rich, very quickly.

But the young man wasn't Mike Krieger or Kevin Systrom.

And the company he created wasn't Instagram.

His name was George Eastman. And the year was 1874.

The company he founded was called Eastman Kodak, and his breakthrough invention was roll film.

Roll film paved the way for the compact cameras of the 20th century and the movie industry—without George Eastman and Kodak film, there would have been no George Lucas and *Star Wars*.

But roll film wasn't *why* Kodak was so successful. What attracted Kodak's original fans was that it offered a solution that satisfied a deep human need: our need to connect, to share our experiences and lives with each other.

Eastman didn't just invent roll film. He developed a point-and-click camera that came preloaded with film. He developed a processing system that meant you could drop off your camera at a drugstore then get your pictures back developed, plus your camera reloaded with film.

He employed "design thinking"—thinking from the "whole human experience," how it fitted together, how it looked, and how it felt.

Eastman's innovation made it simpler, easier, and much more fun.

Later, Kodak developed filters so its users could style their images, and carousels, so they could share with friends and family at home. It all added to the experience.

By 2010, Eastman was long gone from Kodak. And the company he had founded had long lost touch with his original social mission.

The reason Krieger and Systrom were so successful was because they started where Eastman had started. It wasn't about designing the cleverest tech, but how best to satisfy the social needs of those for whom they were intended.

Eastman's original slogan was "You press the button, we do the rest." If he'd been starting up in 2010, and visiting the Borobudur temple in Java, he wouldn't have thought about film. He'd have thought about how to use his iPhone, and develop an app.

4. How to be a billionaire in three easy moves: part 2

"Photography is not just about creating images—it is my window to experiencing the world and sharing relationships with people"

Diana Kim, The Homeless Paradise project

In the autumn of 1973, Steven Sasson was a graduate electrical engineer itching to ride the new technical wave. At university, much of the teaching had been about analogue electronics, but digital circuitry and silicon chips were the new thing, and like any good geek he was keen to get involved with what was new and emerging.

Like a lot of ambitious young engineers, he'd wanted to work for one of the companies that had inspired him as a kid, so he was excited when he landed a job at Eastman Kodak's labs in Rochester, New York.

By the time Sasson arrived at Kodak, the company was firmly established as the world's biggest photography brand, dominating the supply chain from film stock through to processing. Kodak had a whopping 90 percent share of the film market and camera sales in the United States.

But Sasson was no photography buff. Like George Eastman, he was fired by a curiosity about how he might improve things through the application of new technology.

The first project he was given was to explore the potential of a new piece of microelectronic widgetry called a "charged-coupled device," or CCD, that could convert light patterns into electrical signals. The reason Kodak's senior engineers gave the new technology to an inexperienced new graduate was quite simple—they weren't really interested in technology that turned light into electricity. The vast bulk of Kodak's revenues came from film and photographic paper, so they were interested in using light to make these work effectively, not to make electrical signals.

Sasson was left alone, and he became curious as to how he might store the signals that the CCD produced. The answer soon showed up in the form of digitisation, turning the analogue signals into numbers, which he then stored on magnetic tape.

By 1975, Sasson had developed what was essentially the world's first digital camera. It weighed more than 8 pounds, had only 0.01 megapixel resolution, and it took over 20 seconds to record the grainy black-and-white image to a magnetic tape. But it was a beginning.

Sasson had learned at university about Moore's law, a simple equation by which the emergence of new technology could be gauged. Applying the basic principles of Moore's law suggested that with the predicted advances in memory storage and other components, a commercially viable product would be possible by the end of the century.

He started to hawk his prototype around marketers and product developers in the company, but no one was really interested. Kodak's whole business model was based on film and photographic paper, and its revenues from this had just topped $10 billion a year, and were rising fast. What was the point of a product that didn't contribute to this way of working? What was more, the general consensus was that people would never want to look at images on a screen.

Kodak patented the technology, and did what many incumbent companies do at a time like this: they took a watching brief, meaning that they kept a keen eye on new technological developments while continuing to focus most of their effort, energy, and innovation on their core revenue-earning business.

Kodak's revenues peaked at $16 billion in 1996. By then, the company had two-thirds of the global photography market and was the fifth most valuable brand in the world, worth over $30 billion. It was also beginning to make a good return on its patent for the digital camera by licensing the technology to others—this included mobile phone companies as well as camera makers.

This is where the fundamental flaw of a "watching brief" becomes apparent. By now, Kodak was well and truly disconnected from the social mission that had fired George Eastman. As far as the company was concerned, it was in the business of selling film; thus, any information that came to them was looked at through that highly polarised lens.

While other companies started to grapple with the mind-bending possibilities and challenges that digital cameras afforded, learning quickly as they went, Kodak looked at how it could maximise its revenue from film. The result was the Advanced Photo System (APS), introduced in late 1996. What Kodak tried to do was bring some of the functionality of digital photography to old-school film. It was a neat and clever system, but it had two crucial flaws: First, it wasn't instant—you still needed to send your film off for processing. Second, it was expensive.

If Kodak's attention had been on its original social mission—capturing and sharing moments as simply and easily as possible—it would have seen that its APS technology was a backward step. But as a company in the business of selling film, all it saw was the opportunity to generate more revenue.

As the new millennium rolled in, the photography market rapidly started tipping toward digital. Companies that had taken the time to experiment and understand the potential of the new technology started to introduce innovative products. In June 2000, Samsung released a mobile phone in South Korea that could take pictures. Four months later, Sharp brought out a phone in Japan that could take pictures and send them.

APS never took off. By 2001, the cool kids were interested in digital cameras; they could see their images in the moment and didn't have to pay a cent for the privilege.

Kodak finally stopped making APS cameras in 2004 and started trying to chase the new digital game.

In 2007, the patent on the digital camera ran out, cutting off what had become a critical revenue stream. The company did its best to develop digital products, but by now decades of watching rather than experimenting meant that what had once been one of the most innovative companies in the world could only at best come up with me-too products that no one seemed to care about. Revenues shrivelled.

In February 2012, just two months before Facebook bought Instagram for $1 billion, Kodak filed for Chapter 11 bankruptcy protection in the United States. A company that just 15 years earlier had virtually owned the global photography market was essentially out of business.

Kodak's story is a dramatic one—but also an archetypical case study of why large companies fail in times of transformation. It is why Nokia, a company that owned the mobile phone market in the later 1990s, with seemingly bulletproof products, failed within a decade. It is why the American retailers Blockbuster and Borders seemed just to disappear overnight. It is why the East India Company, a mighty pan-national institution that once ran more than half the world's trade, went bust in just a few decades. It is what underpinned the global financial crisis. It is why many of today's corporations won't exist in 10 years' time.

Kodak had massive resources and, in theory, a deep insight into its global market. It should have been able to knock out something like Instagram as a side project. With its size and resources, it would have been a piffling investment. The reason it didn't, though, was because it had become obsessed with what it did rather than why it did it. It had become preoccupied with getting people to consume more of its products rather than why they actually wanted to take photographs.

In 1995, Clayton Christensen, a professor at the Harvard Business School, introduced the term "disruptive innovation" in his book *The Innovator's Dilemma*. What Christensen was referring to in his book's title was how, at certain points in history, the emergence of new and radical technologies has totally disrupted established business models and businesses—in some cases, completely sweeping them away. Exactly what happened to Kodak.

As the twin forces of digital technology and globalisation have shaken up and disrupted just about every aspect of our lives in the 21st century, disruptive innovation has become the rallying cry of a generation. Everywhere you look, books and articles are trumpeting this new religion; disruption is the means to success, fame, and fortune.

Emotive as it is as a concept, though, compelling speakers at conferences to thump the lectern and use big bold fonts, disruptive innovation is not what made Kevin Systrom and

Mike Krieger so spectacularly successful with Instagram.

In fact, it couldn't be further from it.

The subtitle of Christensen's book—"When New Technologies Cause Great Firms to Fail"—points to why. What Christensen was shedding light on was not the source of the innovation, but its side effect: why great firms fail, not why these new innovations take off.

Disruption isn't the source of the kind of innovation that propelled Instagram from start-up to half a billion users and a billion-dollar valuation in two years. It was the side effect.

The original roll-film technology that Eastman invented was, as Christensen noted, spectacularly disruptive to the incumbent industry. It wasn't just the makers of photographic plates that went under; portrait painters, illustrators, and music hall performers all began to find themselves out of work.

The movie *Mr. Turner* ends with the eminent English Victorian landscape painter having his portrait taken with the new camera tech that Eastman had created, and realising his time has come.

But what made Eastman's innovation so successful was that it made it easier for people to take part.

It was "participatory innovation".

Suddenly, instead of having to be an expert painter, with a studio, a whole host of material and deep technical skills, it was easy to get involved, thanks to Kodak.

Participatory innovation is the source of breakthrough and disruption.

The summer after the Second World War ended, an American inventor named Edwin Land took a vacation with his family. Land was already a very successful man. Back in 1926, when still an 18-year-old student, Land had a moment similar to Eastman's in Santo Domingo. He had been walking down Broadway in New York City, perhaps a little the worse for wear, when the bright lights from the new advertising billboards on Times Square dazzled him. He stumbled into the road and was nearly knocked over by a passing vehicle.

New York City was at the forefront of electrification, and all of a sudden bright lights seemed to be everywhere. His near-death experience made him realise how disruptive flaring, bright lights were going to be.

Land's great invention was the polarising lens, and the company he founded was called Polaroid. Polaroid's filters quickly found applications both with sunglasses makers and with Kodak. When America joined the Second World War, Polaroid filters were used in pilots' sunglasses and in bombsights—a Polaroid filter was fitted to the Norden sight that was used to drop the atomic bomb over Hiroshima.

By 1946, Land was a wealthy man. The war was over and there was a new sense of hope and possibility in the air, so he decided to take his wife and young daughter on a vacation. On the first day on the beach, he wanted to capture the moment, and took a picture of his three-year-old daughter playing in the sand. She was delighted, jumping up and down with excitement and wanting to see the result. But her excitement soon turned to disappointment when Land told her that she'd have to wait days for the picture to be returned from the developer. What had been a glorious moment quickly turned to gloom.

What marked Land out right up to the end of his life was that he was first and foremost an innovator, not a businessman. What he saw in his daughter's reaction was a nuanced version of the social need that Eastman had experienced—the need not just to capture and share moments, but to be able to share them in real time.

Land went back to Polaroid and worked night and day. The solution he eventually came up with was radical for a company whose core competence was optical filters. He invented a camera with instant film.

The Polaroid instant camera was an amazing, quirky piece of tech, but what it made it so successful was that it allowed people to participate in capturing and sharing their experiences with each other in the moment. It took away the time lag, meaning you could do it in real time.

Land's innovation wasn't disruptive, it was counter-disruptive—it made it easier to participate and take part in capturing and sharing the moment. So immediate, it became part of the experience. It enhanced it.

Participatory innovation is about asking a series of questions: how can we make it easier—simpler, quicker, cheaper—to participate? How can we make it better, more intuitive, more fun? How can we make the experience more seamless? How can we make it more social, interactive, creative? How can we make it safer and more secure?

Participatory innovation is where Eastman thought from, and it is where Land thought from. If it had been where the execs of Kodak in the 1990s had thought from, when they had the patent for the digital camera in their back pocket, they would never have launched APS.

Once you start to look through the lens of participatory innovation, a lot of things make sense.

Instagram makes it easier to participate in sharing our experiences with each other. Google makes it easier to participate in search and finding unbiased information. eBay makes it easier to participate in the process of buying and selling stuff. Snapchat makes it easier to participate in goofing around—especially when you are stuck in a dull office wondering why the hell you are there. The Apple Mac, coupled with a package like Logic Pro, makes it easier to participate in making music; YouTube in sharing and watching the videos; Airbnb in renting out and finding a nice place to stay; Tinder in... well, you know what.

The fast-growing wellbeing movements like road cycling, yoga, CrossFit, and Tough Mudder are all participatory.

Participatory innovation is having the same impact on makers and creators that mechanisation had on the skilled textile workers we now call the Luddites. Inevitably, the formerly privileged status of both groups has been sacrificed to the changing times. Yet this participatory innovation has provided the means for a lot more people to participate, without the need for expensive equipment or certain skills. It removes constraints on access and distribution. The result is a dramatic increase in the number of people who can take part, but, conversely, a decrease in the value of the things they make or sell. This is the changing landscape of social economics.

The consumer economy is based on generating value from products and content; the social economy, from participation and tools.

5. Generation why

"We live in a world where there is more and more information, and less and less meaning"

Jean Baudrillard, *Simulacra and Simulation*

In early 2012, a teaser for a new HBO series, *The Newsroom*, showed up on YouTube. The clip contained the opening scene, in which the central character, a TV news anchor named Will McAvoy, played by 58-year-old actor Jeff Daniels, is on the panel of an American political talk show. It opens with the panel being asked by a 20-year-old woman student, "What makes America the greatest country in the world?" The first two panel members give stock answers, but when it comes to McAvoy's turn he takes a moment, collects himself, then launches into a searing monologue that is clearly designed to lay out his role as 'maverick alpha male' in the series.

In a rousing presidential manner that not only silences his host but galvanises the crowd, McAvoy first derides the question, reeling off all the reasons America isn't the greatest country in the world, then derides the woman, calling her a "sorority girl", and finally derides her generation: "You, nonetheless, are without a doubt, a member of the WORST-period-GENERATION-period-EVER-period, so when you ask what makes us the greatest country in the world, I don't know what the fuck you're talking about!"

When the first episode aired in June 2012, you could almost hear the cheers of America's fifty-somethings across the country. It was a monologue that not only showed the background of series writer, Aaron Sorkin, a man well-practised in writing presidential-style rhetoric, from his time working on the *West Wing*, but also told you a lot about the generation that both Sorkin and his main character come from. McAvoy's monologue highlighted the frustrations of the generation to which both the actor and the programme creator belonged: the baby boomers, those born in the period between the end of the Second World War and the early 1960s.

The generation McAvoy was deriding was initially known as "generation Y", a not particularly imaginative label signalling its position following generation X, but over the last decade it has become known as "the millennials"—those born after 1980, who have grown up in the era of globalisation and the Internet. It is a generation that has often been accused of being selfish, disinterested, narcissistic and lazy by parents, social commentators and the mainstream media. McAvoy's monologue also pointed to another prejudice of the time: that they were politically naïve.

Now it is not unusual for older generations to criticise younger generations, especially in times of social, economic and political turbulence.

It is also pretty much always the case that while their frustrations and fears are valid, the conclusions they draw are way off the mark.

And so it was here.

At the time *The Newsroom* came out, the aftershocks of the

global financial crisis were rippling through America, a period that, with hindsight, marked the beginnings of the crossover period between the old economic order and the new.

In the introduction I included a diagram laying out the three phases of societal transformation. On paper they can look logical and orderly. The reality, though, is often messy, traumatic, and bewildering. This is why the experience is such an emotional rollercoaster.

Disruption creates confusion. People become disorientated and scared. When things we thought were immutable start to fail, we grasp for easy answers, often looking for someone or something to blame, but what we are often doing is reacting to symptoms, not root causes.

As I mentioned in the introduction, a 2011 study by the Career Advisory Board in the United States revealed that while older managers saw the millennial generation as being driven by money and status, the millennials themselves clearly expressed a very different motivation.

Nearly three-quarters of those surveyed between 21 and 31 years of age said that having a career with a sense of meaning was most important to them.

The boomers were not wrong about the symptoms they were seeing. It was the conclusions many of them were drawing about them that were incorrect. What was being interpreted as apathy about engaging in rhetorical politics and corporate hoo-ha was actually a quiet but very profound reaction to a system that many young people didn't just see as flawed, but as not working for them at all.

A study a year later from the American National Society of High School Scholars asked 9,000 of its top students and recent graduates which company or organisations they wanted to work for. Of the 200 different organisations cited, the one that came out on top was not a high-profile Wall Street firm, a top legal partnership, or a management consultancy. It was not a glamorous media company. Or a funky high-tech outfit.

It was St Jude Children's Research Hospital, a pioneering, not-for-profit hospital that treats children with cancer and other serious illness.

The survey shows that what a large proportion of young people today consider most important is that their lives and careers should have some real meaning—that they should be about helping others, essentially about something greater than either themselves or just money.

It would be easy to interpret this result as meaning that millennials are primarily interested in working for the public service, non-profits, and "worthy causes", but while this is the case for some, it isn't the point. You need to dig a little deeper into the data.

What the data shows is that they are interested in working for businesses and organisations that are up to something they see as worthwhile, that aligns with their values, and where they can directly see a relationship between what they do and some useful impact in the world.

This doesn't have to mean not-for-profit. John is a 32-year-old engineer working for an oil and gas company that operates in Papua New Guinea. His job is helping to build finder wells in the jungle—on the surface, a job that doesn't seem to fit with what worthy purposeful work might look like.

But that isn't how John sees his work. I met John at a symposium on sustainability, where we were on a panel to talk about the social impact of oil companies in emerging countries. It was a pretty hostile audience, but what John didn't do was try to apologise for the industry he worked in—in fact, he agreed it was an industry that needed to change.

What John spoke about showed he was interested in way more than just getting gas that would be sold for dollars out of the ground. As an engineer, he saw an interesting challenge in looking at how to extract hydrocarbons with as little impact as possible in an environmentally sensitive area. But what really interested him was a bigger mission: helping a fledgling and highly shaky country to develop local capability and people, both as engineers and advocates for a fair society. He spent time working in local schools, mentoring local graduate engineers, ensuring his teams worked to the highest-possible environmental standards, and working with local contract staff to improve their approach to health and safety. What is more, he engaged deeply with the company he worked for. It is hard to do business in PNG without getting into the murky world of kickbacks to local politicians, so he was actively involved in learning how to operate within the culture of the country while standing for principles that are important to him. The most striking thing about talking to him was that he wasn't interested in ideology or in taking some moral high ground; he was interested in actually being at the front line of change.

"It would be easy just to sit back in North America, blowing air about this and that, but being here has helped me realise just how difficult it is to live by your principles in the real world, and also what it takes to do that. It's frustrating and slow, but highly rewarding every time we get a win… Why I work for the company I do is because they are committed to this place, to working safely and ethically, and while they are not perfect, I know they mean it and, more importantly, I know that I contribute to that."

Given that St Jude Children's Research Hospital came out on top of the list of millennials' most desirable place to work, it is worth taking a look at what might be so attractive about that organisation. St Jude's is a paediatric hospital and research facility based in Memphis, Tennessee. It was set up in 1962 by the Lebanese-American comedian Danny Thomas. When Thomas was struggling early in his career, he made a vow that if he ever found success he would open a shrine dedicated to St Jude Thaddeus, the patron saint of hopeless causes. This wasn't just the desperate prayer of someone wanting to cut a deal with God for fame and fortune; he meant it. As his career began to take off, Thomas set about delivering on his promise, spending years raising the funds and connecting with the people he needed to realise his vision.

Thomas opened St Jude's with a clear social purpose that "No child should die in the dawn of life," and a mandate that "no one should be turned away, regardless of race, religion or ability to pay." Since opening, St Jude's has consistently stayed true to this social purpose, treating tens of thousands of children with cancer and other catastrophic diseases, many of them poor and without health insurance. In 1996, Dr Peter Doherty of St Jude's immunology department, was a co-recipient of the Nobel Prize in Physiology or Medicine. What makes St Jude's an extraordinary place is not just the vision and efforts of its founder, but the fact that, to this day, the hospital and those who work for it and support it deliver on that vision. If you work at St Jude's, you know you are making a difference in the world, and working for an organisation that means and does what it says.

The millennial generation's lack of interest in their predecessors' way of life is actually a searing indictment of how empty and meaningless they see it has become. Why would they sign up to work for a company that only exists to make money for its shareholders, that doesn't really give a damn about its employees or the environment? (And, no, the fact you have a Corporate Social Responsibility program doesn't cut it—we mean, really.) Why would they engage with a political system that has been seen to fail to deliver on its promises over and over again, that is so full of the kind of rhetoric that Sorkin favours, but so poor on delivery? What is great about the millennials is that they are a generation that has developed a highly-tuned bullshit detector.

The millennials are the Internet generation, and that has made a profound difference to how they think and operate. Whereas the boomers were brought up in a period when network TV was king and pioneering journalists in Vietnam and, later, Watergate changed public opinion, the millennials have been able to compare what is pumped at them via broadcast media with what people are saying on social media, and see how often the talking heads and news channels are left wanting.

While previous generations might have had a queasy feeling about the veneer of spin and gloss that organisations were able to put on their communications, the millennials have been able to tear a hole right through it.

The reason so many millennials seem to their elders not to want to engage is not because they don't care—it's actually because they care a lot, and they can see the system that is being presented to them is flawed and corrupt. They are looking for something else. They seek integrity in their lives, they seek authenticity and genuine purpose. They want to get involved with things that actually matter. They seek organisations that genuinely want to make the world a better and more interesting place.

That is why organisations that truly stand for something, that are out to make a difference, and, most crucially, demonstrate integrity between what they say and what they do, are so important to them. One of the criticisms of millennials by HR managers is that they don't want to take the time to work their way up the organisation. They are right. Millennials want to participate directly in making a difference.

What we are seeing is a paradigm shift. As a generation, the millennials want lives that have purpose, and it's a trend that is increasing the younger they get (as the children who grew up in the global financial crisis and its aftermath come on-stream). They want to engage with others who are up to something, who are authentic and for whom what they do has integrity; in terms of work, this means organisations they can align with, really trust, and feel part of.

Having said all this, looking at this desire for meaning and purpose as a demographic issue doesn't really tell the full story. This is not an issue exclusive to the young.

While the data for young people shows a generation crying out for work and lives that are authentic and have purpose and meaning, this is actually an issue that bleeds across generations. A significant proportion of generation X shares the same concern. This is showing up as mental issues and a sharp rise in suicides, particularly among men, as middle age beckons and life seems empty and devoid of meaning and purpose. What is more, if you look at what lies behind McAvoy's complaint in the *Newsroom,* it is actually the same issue—a character desperately looking to bring meaning to his existence, raging against the dying light. Blaming the younger generation is a smoke screen.

What we are seeing here is not generational, it is societal. We have entered the age of "generation why"—we don't just want, we need to do work we feel makes a difference, to feel affiliated with organisations that are authentic and in whom we can trust, to be engaged in lives that have meaning and purpose.

6. Vision and blindness

"We try never to forget that medicine is for the people. It is not for the profits. The profits follow, and if we have remembered that, they have never failed to appear. The better we have remembered it, the larger they have been"

George Merck

In the summer of 1975, William Campbell made a discovery. Campbell was a research scientist working in the labs of Merck & Co in New Jersey, and he stumbled across one of those things that make research scientists very excited.

Campbell's team were analysing some soil samples they'd received from Japan, and he noticed that one of the microscopic organisms they had isolated in the soil produced a substance that seemed to kill any bacteria near it stone dead. Campbell was a parasitologist by specialisation, and instantly saw the potential for treating parasites in animals. Because the commercial implications of Campbell's discovery were so obvious, it went rapidly into development. The result was a drug called Ivermectin, which turned out to be even more effective than Campbell had hoped. Not only did it kill gastrointestinal worms in one hit, it also killed the flies that caused the infection and horrible sores on the animals in the first place. Ivermectin was so effective, it quickly became the best-selling veterinary drug in the world.

Now if Campbell had just been a jobbing research scientist interested in the development of commercial products, that would have been the end of the story. He could have lived off the prestige of discovering a blockbuster drug for a long time.

But he wasn't. Like all the scientists at Merck's labs in the 1970s, Campbell had been drawn there by a far greater calling than simply developing best-selling drugs. He was part of a community that was up to something far more meaningful to them than that.

What happened next not only shows the power that businesses driven by an unshakable social mission have to make a massive difference in the world, but how it contributes to their long-term profitability and success. While, a couple of hundred miles up north, Steven Sasson was unsuccessfully trying to get his senior managers at Kodak interested in his digital camera, things went very differently at Merck.

Merck's research setup had been intentionally modelled on a university research lab rather than a traditional commercial facility. Scientists were encouraged to be curious, to talk and discuss ideas together, often over a coffee in the social areas. There was passion and energy and a pervasive sense of common purpose. What marks such cultures out is how they balance collaboration with competition. On the one hand, there is a sense of wanting to strive and achieve, and on the other, to share and help each other out.

A couple of years after his initial discovery, Campbell struck up a conversation with one of his colleagues, Mohammed Aziz. Aziz was an infectious disease expert who had previously worked for the World Health Organisation in Africa. One of the diseases Aziz was particularly concerned about was a condition called river blindness.

River blindness was an especially nasty condition that in 1978 affected tens of millions of people in sub-Saharan Africa and Latin America. It was caused by tiny parasitic worms that entered the human bloodstream when people were bitten by black flies. The initial symptoms were a blistering of the skin and a profound itching. The itching became so unbearable that some people had been known to commit suicide. Over time, the bacteria also destroyed the optical tissue in the eye, leading to blindness.

As the two scientists spoke, they realised that river blindness had a lot in common with the parasitic infections that Ivermectin was so good at combatting in animals. It was one of those "aha" moments that emerge out of small gatherings of enthusiasts; both scientists saw it.

There was one very big issue, though. What was very obvious—especially to Aziz, with his WHO experience—was that the potential recipients of the drug wouldn't be able to afford to pay for it. Neither would their countries. The countries where river blindness was prevalent were all impoverished, and the people who caught it were often in the poorest country areas—they were the poorest of the poor, with no access to money to buy medicines.

But this didn't stop Campbell and Aziz. They went to make a case to the head of research, Roy Vagelos.

Now if Merck were a normal company, this is where the conversation should have stopped. Vagelos's job was to qualify what his staff should and shouldn't spend their time and the company's resources on. Merck was a stock market-listed company with shareholders to worry about. Spending what would most likely amount to hundreds of millions of dollars on developing a product that people couldn't afford to pay for wasn't exactly commercially astute. In fact, it was a potentially no-win situation. If they successfully developed the drug and tried to sell it, even at cost, they would be accused of being a big commercial company exploiting the poor, and if they sold it for what people could afford, which was pretty much nothing, they would be running at a massive loss.

But Vagelos green-lighted the project. It was a decision that would lead to the development of a drug that would alleviate the suffering of tens of millions of people and pretty much wiped out river blindness, but it was also a decision that, at the time, made no commercial sense.

It is therefore a moment that is well worth looking at. Because it is the kind of moment that marks out extraordinary organisations from everyone else. The myriad decisions that employees make in moments like this are what drives performance. In a normal company, the only decision Vagelos could have made was "no," but at Merck & Co, it was the other way around—there was no way he could simply say no to the proposal he had been presented with, because of how the company had been set up.

Merck & Co was established in the United States in 1891 when the German industrialist George Merck Sr moved his family to New Jersey to set up an American subsidiary of his family's chemical company. It was his son, though, who transformed it in the 1920s into the organisation that allowed Roy Vagelos and many others like him to make the kind of day-to-day decisions that would not only lead to the development of a whole host of pioneering medicines, but also make Merck the most commercially successful pharmaceutical company on the planet.

George Merck Jr was brought up in Llewellyn Park, a leafy

garden suburb in New Jersey. Two of his boyhood friends there were the sons of the legendary innovator Thomas Edison. The three boys used to hang out at Edison's lab, and the benevolent Edison spent some time showing them around.

Merck became fascinated by the power of scientific research. He worked hard and was on his way to study for a doctorate in Germany when the First World War broke out, so instead he went to work for his father's chemical company in New Jersey. As happened with many of his generation, the carnage of that war left its mark on him, probably much more so for him as an American with German roots. The war ruptured the relationship between America and Germany, and Merck & Co broke its ties with the company in Germany. Merck became a man with a strong desire to make a difference.

When he took over Merck in 1920, he did something that marks out the leaders of all extraordinary companies. Instead of simply steering the company forward as a commercial concern, he decided that Merck would stand for something far bigger and more important than simply developing and selling chemicals. He had seen what happened in the trenches in the First World War. He declared that the mission of Merck & Co was "the alleviation of disease and suffering"—something the world desperately needed after the appalling ravages of the war.

"We try never to forget that medicine is for the people," he wrote in a letter to his early new hires. "It is not for the profits. The profits follow, and if we have remembered that, they will have never failed to appear."

From then on, everything he did was with this guiding principle in mind. In 1929, he established a research laboratory, very much along the lines of what he had learned from Edison, with a mandate to operate like a top university research department—led by research, not profit.

In 1935, Merck spoke at the American Chemical Society, compelling them to follow his example and invest more in research: "Our success in fighting the battle against disease and suffering will be measured by the net addition we make to the sum of life-saving knowledge for the benefit of all mankind, and it is in the attainment of the utmost and speediest advances toward that end that industry and the medical profession will find themselves so essential to each other." The seeds of the modern pharmaceutical industry were sown.

The best and brightest research scientists flocked to work in Merck's labs. Merck & Co became a honeypot for pioneering research scientists drawn to the company's social mission. Merck had taken a stand. The worthwhile and altruistic nature of that stand triggered a social retrovirus that started to spread out way beyond the edges of the company—into hospitals, GPs, university research labs, and, because of the way scientists exchange ideas, even other pharmaceutical companies. Anyone who had that fire in their belly to do something to alleviate disease and suffering was affected by it.

Merck made his company a pioneering cause. It was a stand that people identified with deeply and personally, something they were prepared to put themselves on the line for. It fostered a collaborative culture that was intensely innovative, as everyone's focus was on the same end goal.

With this as the pervasive conversation, the actions of Campbell, Aziz and Vagelos make perfect sense. They were operating completely consistently with Merck's social mission.

Vagelos made his decision in 1978—21 years after Merck's death—which shows the lasting power of an authentic stand. Many companies that are started by charismatic and powerful leaders go into a tailspin when they leave or pass away. But Merck's guiding purpose lived on so powerfully in the pervasive ethos of the organisation that Vagelos was empowered to make the decision he did.

There is a strong correlation between making your primary purpose the fulfilment of a social mission like Merck's and elevated commercial results—but not one of direct cause and effect. With the non-linear mathematics of the late 20th century, we began to understand how this worked—which is why enlightened VCs were prepared to back socially driven companies like Google and Facebook with hundreds of millions of dollars when they had no immediate business model—but in the 1930s, this new maths was still in its infancy. Merck was way ahead of his time.

It takes brave leadership and leaps of faith to focus your business on the fulfilment of a social mission. It requires the establishment of an unshakable commitment to an ethos that not only gives leaders like Vagelos the permission to make bold decisions, but also has them understand the consequences if they do not. Everyone needs to buy into it. You either stand for something, or you do not. It is a binary proposition.

This is why trying to lead a company whose primary purpose is the fulfilment of a social mission using traditional "cost control" accounting methods doesn't work. It needs the application of non-linear logic (which we will come to later). In a company that was managed solely on spreadsheets, Vagelos's decision would have been career suicide. In a company with an ethos as strong and pervasive as Merck's in the 1970s, it would have been career suicide not to make the decision. He knew those up the line were with him, and those working for him were counting on him.

Merck spent more than $200 million developing a cure for river blindness, producing a drug called Mectizan. Vagelos went on to become CEO of the company. In 1987, he announced

Merck would donate Mectizan to a not-for-profit to treat river blindness. The result was the formation of Mectizan Donation Program, an independent body managed by the Task Force for Global Health.

By 2011, more than 30 million people a year were receiving Mectizan, and more than a billion treatments had been administered by the Mectizan Donation Program. This is the legacy of George Merck's stand, and the commitment of those like Campbell, Aziz, and Roy Vagelos, who signed up for the cause—the alleviation of disease and suffering, in this case in the lives of tens of millions of human beings who would have otherwise been blinded and scratching themselves to death. River blindness has all but been eradicated as a serious disease. In 2015 William Campbell was awarded the Nobel Prize in Physiology or Medicine in recognition of his contribution.

What is equally significant, though, is that throughout the period of its development of Mectizan, Merck & Co went from strength to strength. By the early 1990s, it was the most successful and valuable pharmaceutical company on the planet.

7. Why we do what we do

"We feel we choose. But we don't"

Professor Patrick Haggard, Institute of Cognitive Neuroscience

Neuroscience is no new thing. Fossil remains that date back to the neolithic period show evidence of a surgical procedure called "trepanation", the drilling of small holes in the skull to relieve cranial pressure. It is a procedure that is still used today. Granted, punching a hole in the skull with a sharp rock wasn't exactly microsurgery, but it was a start, and carbon dating shows that some of those who were operated on lived for quite a while after the procedure—so it looks as if it might have worked.

It wasn't until around 400 BC in ancient Greece, though, that scientists started to believe that the brain was where we did our thinking. Before that, the popular belief was that our conscious thoughts came from our heart and gut. The physician Hippocrates, who is generally regarded as the founding father of modern medicine, was instrumental in shifting expert opinion to the belief that the brain is the centre of cognitive thought.

In the two millennia since Hippocrates, our understanding of how the brain and our cognitive processes work has developed massively, but one of his original assumptions remained in place until the 1970s: the belief that the brain was a solid, immutable object in which thought processes went on.

In the late 1970s, research started to show that Hippocrates' assumption was incorrect. Improvements in the ability to monitor the brain's detailed electrical activity allowed researchers to see that when groups of neurons fired at the same time, they would start to bond and mesh—coining the phrase "neurons that fire together, wire together"—and actually changed the physiology of the brain. The more bundles of neurons were fired together, the more they became physically enmeshed. Conversely, enmeshed neurons that weren't fired over time would loosen their bond. What this showed was the brain was not hardwired, but could be conditioned and reconfigured far more than had previously been thought—a phenomenon that became known as "neuroplasticity".

Neuroplasticity explains how we become conditioned to do things: we learn, we do, we learn, we do, and, as this happens, the bonding between the critical neurons becomes more refined and physically connected. It also explains why we find it so hard to let go of habits we have decided aren't good for us; once a bond is made, it doesn't unravel easily.

So far, so logical, but this is where the story takes a critical and unsettling twist.

In the mid-1980s, Benjamin Libet, a neurophysiologist at the University of California in San Francisco, embarked on a series of experiments designed to measure the time difference between the triggering of enmeshed neurons. He was interested in quantifying the gaps between when a decision to act was made and when the associated action was triggered.

Libet's results were not at all what he expected. In fact, they were so startling that they challenged the way most of our brains have become wired.

What Libet found was that the neurons responsible for a

decision to take an action were actually fired a few hundred milliseconds after the neurons responsible for triggering the action itself.

This is a mind-blowing finding—and might take a moment to process. The neurons that are responsible for a decision to take an action are fired after those responsible for triggering the action itself. What this suggests is that when we think we have made a decision to do something, what we have really done is make a very fast post-rationalisation of why we did it—one that is made so quickly that we are left with the impression we have made a choice. In other words, we act first, think second, but don't realise it. Libet's discovery challenges the whole notion of free will.

After Libet's research was published, his methods of measurement were disputed—perhaps because the results were so potentially disturbing—and his work was gradually banished to the outer edges of research, the grey area where cranks overlap with pioneering science. It wasn't disproved, but it certainly didn't fit with the self-determining paradigm of the time.

In 2008, a team led by John-Dylan Haynes, a neuroscientist at the Max Planck Institute for Human Cognitive and Brain Sciences in Leipzig, Germany, set out to create a more accurate version of Libet's work to see if there was any validity to his claims. The ability to analyse and measure brain activity had improved greatly in the 25 years since the original experiments.

What Haynes's team discovered not only validated Libet's original research but turned out to be a bunker buster. They found that not only were Libet's findings correct, but that the gap between the action being taken and the lagging "decision" was often seconds rather than milliseconds. In the most extreme case, the gap was as long as 10 seconds.

"We think our decisions are conscious," Haynes told *Nature* magazine, when the results were published at the end of 2008. "But these data show that consciousness is just the tip of the iceberg."

Now it is easy to oversimplify what is actually an extremely complex process. What Haynes's research suggests isn't that we have no control over the actions we take—it is possible to override our immediate reactions, particularly in complex situations that require exploration. What it does show, though, is that in many stimulus-response situations, our actions are not governed by our conscious thoughts.

While in many ways this finding is deeply troubling, it does bring with it some respite for those of us who have struggled with trying to change our behaviours in areas like exercise, diet, and lifestyle—areas where we know what the right things to do are, but just can't seem to do them.

Haynes's research helps us begin to understand why organisations that are built on a deep and unshakable sense of purpose are so successful. If the majority of our actions are not governed by our conscious mind, then they are instead being governed by our unconscious. Whereas our conscious mind is able to flex and pivot, based on new facts and circumstances, the values and beliefs that govern our unconscious are built up and layered over time. What is more, our unconscious is influenced by the culture we are living in—what the psychoanalyst Carl Jung called "the collective unconscious".

What we see in organisations where there is a belief in a bigger game, something meaningful and real, and a pervasive ethos that supports it, is that the majority of the actions those in the organisations take are in service of that purpose—whether they are in plans or not. People are led by their unconscious, and the collective unconscious, to take actions that will forward the game, often going way above and beyond what might be seen as "normal"—as we saw with Roy Vagelos at Merck & Co. They don't need managing or controlling. In fact, removing overly constraining command and control structures actually frees them to participate even more fully—to use their own ingenuity, creativity, and commitment to deal with things as they emerge. Their drive comes from within.

When George Merck shared with people his stand for Merck & Co, he engaged people on an emotional level—it was about alleviating human suffering, something that touched people deeply and personally as a reason to go to work. What is more, he backed up his words with deeds: the creation of the labs, constant praise for brilliant science, supporting projects that didn't immediately suggest bottom-line gain. There was an authenticity and integrity to his stand. This is what impacts our unconscious. Merck set up his labs based on a university model to encourage people to focus their research primarily on the alleviation of human suffering. The whole organisation was oriented around this social mission.

If Vagelos had made his decision on whether to invest in developing a cure for river blindness on logic—market intelligence and cost-benefit spreadsheets—the project wouldn't have gone through the first gate.

Instead, his actions were governed by what he *felt* was right—what was generated from his unconscious set of values and beliefs that had been shaped over time by working at Merck & Co. He didn't have to "think", he unconsciously "knew".

This sense of knowingness rippled way beyond the boundaries of the company into the wider collective unconscious. At the time that Vagelos backed the river blindness project, more than 50 percent of the general public believed the pharmaceutical industry was doing a good job in its contribution to society. What

Merck & Co and its peers were doing jived with something deep in many human beings—what they were doing struck people as meaningful, significant, and had a higher purpose.

In the mid-1990s, though, the pharmaceutical industry began to change. In many ways, the industry became a victim of its own success. Analysts and investors became less tolerant of a model, where, for every massively successful product, there were many others that went nowhere. They wanted more big wins, they wanted better returns. A new discipline called "pharmacoeconomics" emerged that switched the focus from efficacy to economic return. Drugs were flipped so side effects became their selling point, moving them from one market to another—an anti-obesity drug that made people feel better was potentially far more lucrative than an antidepressant that also helped them lose weight.

In 1995, Merck & Co's board, encouraged by consultants, decided they needed to change the company's mission to something more focused on the bottom line. Their mission became "being a top-tier growth company".

What this did was create a dissonance between what the company stood for and why its employees and those it interacted with in the medical and health-care community were drawn to it in the first place.

Expecting scientists to be excited about being part of "a top-tier growth company" is like the Glazers sitting down with the Manchester United football team and expecting them to get excited about cash-flow. Football players play football to engage in what for them is a deadly serious game, to beat the opposition, to entertain the fans. Research scientists are not much different. It is just a different game they play. "Top-tier growth" might be important to the analysts and investors, but it is not what drives the enthusiasts and fans who make great organisations work.

The new mission didn't align with the reasons the scientists were there.

The result was that the company maintained its position as number one pharmaceutical company for a couple more years, but then growth slowed and it lost its top spot, and never recovered it. Two years is the sort of time it takes for the collective unconscious to come to terms with the fact that the prevailing ethos has changed irreparably, for the enmeshed neurons to rewire.

What the rise and fall of Merck & Co shows is the power of the unconscious mind—how we are driven by internal beliefs and attachments, beliefs and attachments that are shaped by our emotional rather than cognitive reaction to what we experience. It shows we are driven far more by how we feel in a moment than what we think.

This phenomenon explains why so much market research isn't accurate. What we saw when Jay was asked about why she chose her iPhone is that actually we don't often really know why we do what we do. We can—and do—post-rationalise it. And this is what shows up in research, especially multiple-choice questionnaires. But the reality is the motivations for many of our actions come from somewhere deep within—core values, beliefs, and emotional attachments that have been grooved in over a long period of time—and we are unconscious to our motivations. We act in accordance with our *felt experience*, not our conscious assessments.

Industries tend to work on a pack mentality, and in the mid-1990s many other pharmaceutical companies followed Merck & Co's lead, shifting the pharmaceutical industry from one focused on alleviating disease to one focused on growth and making profit. You could call this "the curse of best practice".

By 2008, the public perception of the pharmaceutical industry as a positive contributor to society had tanked to a barrel-scraping 15 percent. Instead of being seen as a force for good, the industry was perceived by the public as being obsessed with profits, greed, and driven by questionable ethics.

In the same period, the public's perception of the computer industry, driven by a whole host of pioneering companies, many of which didn't even exist in 1998, had soared—with more than 70 percent of the public seeing it as contributing positively to society. What the public experienced, what seeped into the collective unconscious over time, was tech company after tech company being led by a desire to make something useful and good: Google's drive to make information available to all, Wikipedia's not-for-profit goal of engaging the whole world in sharing knowledge, Facebook connecting people and communities, even Angry Birds out to save you from the tedium of a boring teacher or bus ride home. It was not that these companies were simply out to do good—Silicon Valley is in many ways capitalism at its most raw—but that they were being led by their social mission to make and do something useful and good, rather than the single-minded pursuit of shareholder value and profit.

In October 2013, Merck & Co announced it would be cutting 8,500 jobs and $1.5 billion off its costs. At the same time over in Silicon Valley, high-tech start-ups and giants like Google, Facebook, and Apple were drawing in talent and investment in the same way that Merck had when he opened his labs in 1929.

Just as Kodak fell under the misapprehension that it was in the business of selling film, and the music industry thought it was in the business of flogging disks, so too had Merck & Co fallen under the misapprehension that it was in the business of selling drugs.

8. In the club

"The ambitions for the business were always much bigger than creating a little niche and selling some expensive road cycling gear. The business is all about the sport. I think road cycling is the most beautiful thing in the world, and the toughest sport in the world, and I think it should be the biggest sport in the world…that is the crazy vision that drives me forwards"

Simon Mottram, founder and CEO, Rapha

Coffee once had the kind of reputation that cocaine enjoys today—the fuel of fast living and shifty deals, glamorous or depraved, depending on your point of view. Its rehabilitation started in 1600 when Pope Clement VIII declared it "an acceptable Christian beverage", influenced perhaps by the delights of a caramel *macchiato*, but more likely by Venetian traders who saw coffee's economic potential, and promised to swell the papal coffers. The world's first coffee house was established in Venice in 1629 and quickly became a meeting place for would-be entrepreneurs, merchants, and late-Renaissance geeks. At the time, money lending was banned by the church in Rome, so if you wanted to source some seed capital, the booths at the back of the coffee shop were a good place to look.

Since then, wherever there have been creative and entrepreneurial conversations, coffee has rarely been far away.

In 1688, a group of sailors, hustlers, and shipowners started to congregate at the newly opened Lloyd's Coffee House on the east side of the City of London. The shop was close to the docks, so it had access to the best, freshest coffee that was newly arriving from North Africa and the Middle East. Because of this, and its proximity to both the docks and the city's mercantile centre, it quickly became a place to get the inside scoop on the comings and goings of the merchant ships that were opening up the New World.

A vibrant informal network began to emerge as investors, chancers, and young blades keen to explore the world and make their fortune hooked up. London was only just beginning to emerge as a financial centre, and banking was in its infancy (the first banknote wasn't released until 1695). Lloyd's provided the means to satisfy a critical emerging need of the time—the need for capital investment in what were the high-risk start-ups of the day, speculative voyages to the New World, bringing back valuable spices and all manner of goods. The coffee shop became a place where all sorts of creative ways to borrow money and insure risk could be agreed with a nod and a handshake.

Lloyd's soon became the place to go if you wanted to get involved in the risky but potentially highly lucrative merchant shipping opportunities that the New World afforded. The more people connected with colleagues and business associates, the more Lloyd's became the epicentre for New World business opportunities, which in turn drew others in, a sign that a social retrovirus was now in play.

Three years after it opened, Lloyd's relocated to Lombard

Street in the City of London, home of the fledgling banking system, and the network began to take shape. Financiers started to pay to up take up a permanent place in the building, and a system of membership known as "Lloyd's names" was put in place. Now the retrovirus had really taken hold—Lloyd's had become an intrinsic part of how merchant shipping was financed.

Over the next 300 years, this network gradually grew into what it is today: Lloyd's of London, one of the world's biggest insurance markets, and the largest for maritime reinsurance. In 2012, more than £23 billion of premiums were sold through its market, making a tidy £2.8 billion profit. Lloyd's of London is still fulfilling the original purpose that drew people together in the coffee shops by the docks—connecting investors with high-risk ventures, especially those involving mercantile ships.

Ten years after Lloyd's first opened its doors, and about half a mile west, a group of young stockbrokers who had been thrown out of the Royal Exchange for being rowdy started to meet up at Jonathan's Coffee House nearby. The Royal Exchange was London's commodity market, and being banned meant the stockbrokers needed to find other means to hustle. So they met to share information and tips. They knew market intelligence was vital and started to pay local street kids to hang around the docks and sniff around for news. John Castaing, a broker from the Royal Exchange who liked to hang out at Jonathan's, started to write up the information on a board on the wall. The board at Jonathan's soon became known as a good place to get the inside scoop on investment trends. That in turn attracted others with a stomach for risk and a desire for a quick return on their investment, adding richness to the information. Jonathan's gradually became known as *the* place to go if you wanted to make a clever early investment in the London commodity markets.

The institution that grew out of that original small gathering at Jonathan's Coffee House is what today is called the London Stock Exchange, one of the largest trading exchanges in the world, turning over more than $5 billion of trades a day.

The networks that grew to become Lloyd's of London and the London Stock Exchange were highly disruptive to the economic order of the day, as northern European protestants, unencumbered by the moral code of Rome, used them to borrow money to invest in trade with the New World. As the economic power shifted north, London became the centre of global trade and Venice started to sink slowly into its canals.

However, like Kodak, Polaroid, and Instagram, the thinking the gatherings at Lloyd's and Jonathan's coffee house were based on was participatory. They were established to help people participate more easily in commerce and trade. They were born out of the desire to satisfy a pressing social need of the time rather than to try to build a business. Once this seed was planted, a community began to grow, with structure emerging bottom-up over time.

Now, nearly 350 years later, and a mile farther west, in Soho—a part of London that was full of brothels in 1688 but is now unashamedly hip—the Rapha Cycle Club is continuing in this tradition. Formed by a small group of men with a fervent passion for road cycling, Rapha has quickly grown into a multimillion-pound business with a phenomenally loyal set of high-spending fans.

The Rapha cycling club is technically a shop that sells gear for road cycling enthusiasts, but it feels a lot more like a coffee shop or meeting place. At a table by the window, three young men are discussing which is the hardest of the mountain stages of the Tour de France. It's an intense debate. The men are all whippet-thin and decked out in the kind of gear favoured by London bike couriers—a combination of elegant retro road cycling gear and hard-wearing street fashion. Small cups of espresso from the club's hipster-run coffee shop sit close at hand.

Over the course of the day, people—mainly men—come and go. What they all have in common is a look that says they ride bikes and take it seriously. They are lean, gaunt, and quite grave, often wearing a cycling cap, and sometimes with the right leg of their skinny jeans rolled up, as they have just hopped off a bike left locked up outside. They browse, they chat, share stories and drink coffee. Sometimes they buy something from one of the racks of exquisitely-styled cycling wear.

They have all the hallmarks of hard-core fans: knowledgeable, obsessive, extremely serious about their passion, and intensely involved. This being northern Europe, there are many tales of gruelling rides in sleet and rain. In fact, there often seems to be a competition for who had the hardest, most unpleasant ride.

Self-actualisation
achieving one's full potential, including creative activities

Esteem needs
prestige, feeling of accomplishment

Belongingness & love needs
intimate relationships, friends

Safety needs
security, safety

Physiolgical needs
food, water, warmth, rest

Rapha was established in 2004, the brainchild of British road cycling enthusiast Simon Mottram. Like the gatherings at Lloyd's and Jonathan's coffee houses, what started out as a small group of intense men with a shared passion has proven highly commercially rewarding. Rapha has seen triple-digit growth for the best part of a decade, and has become one of the hottest and most talked-about niche brands. In 2013, *The Sunday Times* listed it as one of its top 100 fast-track companies. Four years later, in August 2017, the American venture capital company, RZC Investments, bought a majority share of the company, valuing it at over £200 million.

Rapha is a master class in the application of participatory innovation to build a high-value brand with passionate and extremely loyal fans in the emerging new economy.

Towards the end of 2001, Mottram, then working as a freelance branding consultant, gave a presentation at the Luxury Brand Association in London. He used the psychologist Abraham Maslow's classic hierarchy of human needs as a framework.

Maslow's now famous hierarchy was first published in a research paper in 1943. Psychology had emerged as an academic discipline in the second half of the 19th century, part of an explosion of scientific and intellectual growth as the disruptive phase of the Industrial Revolution gave way to social transformation. But Maslow was the first psychologist to focus on what made human beings successful. Prior to this, the discipline had been preoccupied with dysfunction and how to treat it.

Maslow interviewed a hundred highly successful people, including Albert Einstein and Eleanor Roosevelt, and started to build a model of what he found they had in common (he was not considering merely material success, but people he saw as having a profound sense of satisfaction, achievement and fulfilment).

What he realised was that we have a stack of needs as human beings, starting at the bottom with the most basic physiological needs (food, water, shelter, sex), and rising to what he called 'self-actualisation'—what could be called our spiritual needs. The further up the stack we get in terms of having our needs met, the happier and more fulfilled we are.

Mottram used a simplified version of this model in his presentation. The central thrust of his talk was that while we live in an age where the basic "lower-tier" needs of many human beings in developed countries are being met (food, water, shelter, and so on), increasingly, their higher needs are not. He pointed to what he saw as a rapidly expanding gap, and discontent, that was growing between the desire to have these higher needs met and what brands, companies—and even societies—were offering. He also suggested that what was then just the first rumblings of unrest against globalisation was a symptom of this.

It was a clever, forward-thinking presentation—and it is safe to say, on the whole, the audience was pretty underwhelmed. These were brand managers of luxury brands, who were on the one hand comfortable with the way things were, while also still slightly bewildered by the impact that the dot-com boom was having on their industry. They didn't need something else to worry about.

Like many great ideas, Rapha was really the product of a moment in time when a number of things came together. Mottram passionately believed in what he was talking about, and was deeply frustrated by how resigned and closed-minded so many brand managers seemed to be. He was also a keen and active road cyclist. And, finally, he was a pretty snappy dresser.

In the summer after the presentation, he set off on a ride

with some friends and fellow hard-core road bike enthusiasts through the south of France. Designer Luke Scheybeler—who would later become Rapha's creative director—was part of the crew, and he and Mottram started to talk about the possibility of creating a brand for people like themselves. Scheybeler started to take pictures, capturing the aesthetic of small ancient towns, lush poppy fields, and gruelling climbs in the High Pyrrenees. Meanwhile, the group argued long into the nights about the relative merits of Italian and Japanese bike parts. It was a classic example of the kind of conversations fans have—passionate, heated, good-natured and competitive in equal measure—and one in which there was never going to be agreement.

When Mottram looked at his friends, what he saw was a group of 30-something men with a deep commitment and love of road cycling. But he also saw something he had talked about in his presentation. He realised for them it was about far more than just riding bikes. Every night, they talked about the glory days of the Tour de France, the epic battles, the tragic deaths, the thrills and spills. They were steeped in its mythology and heroism. What he also was touched by was how much he and his friends got from being part of a group with this common passion. There was something epic and important about it. He coined a phrase that would become Rapha's guiding principle: "Glory through suffering". That was what they were all about. It wasn't just cycling, it was the heroism and the camaraderie and the individual struggle. Road cycling gave them purpose, it gave them meaning, and it was something they loved to feel part of—satisfying a number of items from the top of Maslow's stack. These were not simply functional human needs. They were emotional, social, and what might be called spiritual needs.

What also frustrated Simon and his friends was how hard it was to get decent cycling clothes. They all had beautifully made and styled Italian bikes, handcrafted with state-of-the-art components that cost upwards of £5,000 in some cases. But they found it really hard to find clothing that both looked good and performed well. The beautifully austere aesthetic from the 1960s and '70s they all loved and yearned for had been blitzed by gaudy, nasty Lycra, covered in logos for mobile phones and Italian dairy products.

Mottram was an instinctive participatory innovator. The opportunity he saw wasn't so much to make cycling clothes as to provide the means for people like himself and his friends to take part in and to feel part of a community with a shared and serious passion. Part of this was about being able to get hold of really well-styled, high-performance clothing that enhanced their ability to participate, both on and off the bike.

Neither Mottram nor Scheybeler had any background in fashion, and they started with minimal funding, raised mainly through their cycling friends. They rented a small space in the back end of an alteration tailor's in North London, and plastered the walls with pictures of road cycling's glory days. They came to work on road bikes, which they stacked in the corner. Everyone they talked to was in some way involved with road cycling.

In fact, to be part of Rapha you had to ride a bike. It was an immersive environment. Product development was undertaken in the same agile, fluid, collaborative manner as the original teams at Kodak and Instagram. Everyone was in it together, united in fulfilling the same purpose; their ride to work through the rain and their collective road cycling obsession was their lab.

They didn't have much development capital—at the start, they all freelanced to pay the bills—so they put together an initial range of only two core products: an austere classic jersey made of hi-tech merino wool and a similarly austere black soft-shell jacket designed for the colder and wetter climes of northern Europe, as these were the items they struggled most to find.

Rather than officially launch or market the product, they instead decided to give the first batch of jackets away to a select group of London's cycle couriers to test—a group seen as the hardest of hard-core riders by many road cyclists. The jacket was highly functional and minimally stylish. Production was limited, and the jerseys and jackets were only made available to the hardest of the hard core. Couriers loved them, and they quickly became much sought-after.

Word began to spread in the cafés and bars where couriers met. Rapha released a limited-edition T-shirt and gave samples to mechanics who worked in some of London's coolest road cycling shops. People came into the store and wanted to know where they could get them. This is where Mottram's luxury-brand experience showed up. Like Apple, Rapha kept, and continues to keep, tight control of its supply chains. When it launched its website, for the first six months there were no photographs of products; just pencil drawings. This stoked curiosity. It was a strategy of attraction not promotion.

All this brought Rapha to the question of how to sell its clothes, and this is where the spirit of the club was born. In his presentation, Mottram had highlighted how the increasing lack of trust and faith that many people now have in mainstream brands, corporations, and governments has left a huge yearning; what Maslow called "the need for affiliation and belonging".

Mottram and Scheybeler didn't want Rapha's products sitting next to horrible Lycra in cycling stores, and they didn't want them perceived as a fashion brand in conventional stores—in fact, they really didn't want them falling into the wrong hands at all. So they decided that instead of selling them in a conventional way, they would host events that drew the kind of cycling fans who were interested in what they were interested in—and, by implication, no one else.

Their first event was an exhibition in the Old Truman Brewery in London's grittily fashionable Shoreditch. Mottram took a large chunk of their tiny seed funding and went to France to source a pile of vintage cycling paraphernalia: old pictures, magazines, and other artefacts. They borrowed some classic road bikes, each one beautifully restored. The exhibition was called "Kings of Pain" and celebrated the glory and suffering of the classic days of the Tour de France. There were a couple of racks with their few samples, but the main focus of the event was on their love of the sport.

The exhibition was a great success, and both the cult and community of Rapha was born. Fellow road cycling enthusiasts turned up, some even brought things along. There were intense conversations, with sharing of stories, and that sense of camaraderie that Mottram and Scheybeler had experienced when they rode through southern France with their fellows. People didn't just come to see; they came to join in. An active community with a shared passion started to form.

Mottram and Scheybeler started to host Rapha participatory events, like the infamous "Smithfield Nocturne", a hard-core night-time race through the rough streets of London's Smithfield Market. Their approach was pure and quirky in equal measure. They bought an old vintage Citroën van and went to the Tour de France, where they sold coffee, creating a sort of pop-up version of Lloyd's and Jonathan's coffee shops—enthusiasts clustered around them.

What Rapha didn't do was contrive marketing events. There was nothing pretend about them. They created authentic situations in which enthusiasts could turn up and participate in their passion for hard-core road cycling—sharing, talking about, and actually riding. As with the vibrant communities that emerged at Lloyd's and Jonathan's, what emerged were relationships, ideas, and connections they couldn't ever have conceived.

Rapha didn't push their brand in stores; people came looking for it. They drove the whole sales side of the business from their website, and each product was highly limited in run. Getting hold of a Rapha product became a badge of honour and, for many, an obsession. Some high-spending professionals became so obsessed with the brand that Mottram invented a brand within a brand called "Imperial Works" (named after the Victorian factory they worked out of) that offered expensive, exclusive products and events only available for those who reached a certain level of spending. They even created a new *de facto* web domain. Rapha.com had been taken, so they used Rapha.cc, the domain name of the Cocos (Keeling) Islands, a tiny cluster of islands with 600 inhabitants in the South Pacific, appropriating it to mean "cycling club". Now every niche cycling brand worth its salt uses .cc.

The keen sense of affiliation and belonging that all this engendered was where the social retrovirus was born—being part of the Rapha community became a really important part of fans' lives. The Rapha logo wasn't so much a brand as a symbol of membership to an exclusive club of like-minded souls, a connection between Rapha fans, who would give each other a knowing nod if they saw each other on a ride.

In the same way that football fans enrol their friends and families, Rapha fans enrolled others they liked to ride and hang out with, either directly or because riders noticed the serious cool-looking riders who wore Rapha and wanted in. Rapha's marketing strategy was very much about attraction rather than promotion.

As the community expanded, so did the scale of their events. Rapha now curates an ongoing series of events in different places around the world called "The Rapha Continental"— tough, epic rides in Europe, America, and Asia, where fans and enthusiasts obsessed with road cycling can meet, ride, and compete together. It is all about being a part and taking part.

Cycling blogs started to discuss the brand, and this is where an important aspect of fanatical affiliations showed itself: Rapha strongly divided opinion. Some cycling fans loved it, others hated it—with one man famously saying he didn't understand why you needed to pay such a lot of money for a rain jacket when you could ride in a plastic bag. Not only did Mottram do nothing to mitigate this backlash, he positively encouraged it.

This "with us or against us" mentality is a critical characteristic of brands that attract fans. It distinguishes them from conventional businesses, where market share is everything and negative reactions and bad press send quivers of panic through the PR department. Fans want to be part of something, but they also want to be in competition with something. There would be no Manchester United without the other teams in the English Premier League. Clubs that are worth being a part of are exclusive—they serve those they are there for, and not anyone else.

Rapha apparel is race-cut, and there are no plus-sized items. It is up to you to put the work in to fit them, rather than them fitting you. It isn't a lifestyle brand, it is a participatory brand—it is for people who put in the miles and are prepared to suffer on their bikes.

In 2013, Rapha pulled off a coup that, just a few years before, might have seemed like a pipe dream. A Rapha shirt was worn by Chris Froome of Team Sky as he won the Tour de France.

A small company that was still operating out of an old sewing machine factory had done the same as Arctic Monkeys when they beat Robbie Williams to the top of the UK charts—in just a few short years, they had seemingly come out of nowhere and usurped the mighty Adidas as the shirt supplier to the winner of the most prestigious road race of them all. Froome was a great climber, and he won the race by dominating in the high mountains—the same mountains that Mottram and his small group of friends had sweated and suffered on, and where the spirit of Rapha was born.

9. The deadly serious game

"It's all in the game, yo. All in the game"

Omar Little, *The Wire*

Driving down Ann Street through Fortitude Valley in Brisbane is a study in how cities organically regenerate themselves. Every large Western city has some version of an area like this, a formerly run-down part of the inner city that is being rebooted one unit at time as offbeat entrepreneurs open quirky bars and specialist shops, attracted by the urban vibe and lower rents. They are areas that have traditionally attracted poorer immigrants for the same reasons—close to the hustle of the city centre and not too expensive. Fortitude Valley—or "the Valley", as it is known locally—has been a draw for people from East Asia for years, originally China, then Vietnam, and now a whole host of countries.

The Internet café where I am sits in the hinterland between the rapidly gentrifying main strip, with its hipster boutiques and indie music venues, and an area that is the closest thing Brisbane has to a red-light district—home to some dodgy-looking clubs, hollow-faced addicts, and dubious massage parlours.

The café is a big, bright space, going back a long way, belying its small, shabby shop front, and it is packed with young Asian kids, all energetically tapping away at keyboards. It is known locally for its ultrahigh-speed Internet connection, a necessity for playing some of the more graphically rich online games, so the place is a magnet for serious gamers.

"Is everyone playing?" I whisper, aware that the room is deadly quiet.

"Pretty much," says Lisa, making no effort to whisper. "That or talking with family back home." She laughs. "But you don't have to whisper. They all have headphones."

"But no one is saying anything."

"They'll be messaging."

I have struck lucky with Lisa. I came to the shop hoping to talk to someone who played a game that I had heard was sweeping the gaming community, but when I arrived I found everyone totally immersed and uninterruptible. Lisa was at the front desk, and when I asked her if she knew anyone who played *Minecraft*, her face lit up.

Lisa is a hip 31-year-old from Taiwan. Like a lot of young Asian women travelling in Australia, she is wearing coloured lenses, so her eyes are a strange opaque dark blue. She has what Taiwanese call a "Loli" look—a mash-up of supermodel, princess and punkette. So she certainly doesn't fit my stereotype of an online gamer—traditionally male, adolescent, or in a suspended state of adolescence, and either obsessed with dungeons and dragons or blowing things to pieces.

But then calling *Minecraft* "a game" doesn't really do it justice. *Minecraft* is what in gaming terms is known as an "open world" or "sandbox", a concept that couldn't be more different in mindset to the high-octane and often mindless shoot-'em-up kind of games. Open worlds are designed to let their participants wander, explore and create things, rather than search out and destroy.

In simple terms, *Minecraft* is a game in which participants can design and build things with others. In old-school terms, it is more like a box of Lego than a game of war. One of the things that has made *Minecraft* so popular is its combination of simplicity and depth. It is really easy to start making things with its building blocks, but the sky's the limit to what you can create if you know how.

Lisa shows me the project she is working on with some friends back home. They are recreating a part of Winterfell from the HBO TV series *Game of Thrones* as part of a huge community that is working on creating the whole of the TV series' mythical world. It is a stunningly complex undertaking.

"I think Taiwan is like the Kingdom of the North," she says with a smile. "And King's Landing is like China."

Minecraft is one of the most successful mass participation games in the world. It has more than 100 million registered users, generating upwards of half a billion dollars in revenue. At any one time, there are 4 to 5 million people playing online at the same time. By the standards of not only the gaming industry, but of all entertainment industries, it is a blockbuster.

But *Minecraft* wasn't created by one of the huge gaming companies that dominate the market. It evolved very differently from large studio products, in a way that is now becoming familiar to us—by an enthusiast at the centre of a small vibrant community of like-minded people. What is more, it was created with virtually no funding.

In 2009, Markus Persson, or "Notch" as he is known in the developer community, was working as a software developer in Stockholm. *Minecraft* started life as a side project he did in his spare time. Software development is pretty taxing on the brain, and Notch was also active on many online communities, so

Minecraft had to be fitted in with a lot of other things.

Its humble beginnings account for some of its simplicity. Notch was a software developer, not a designer, and he didn't have a creative department to fall back on. The characters and world he created were therefore unashamedly rudimentary and low-res. This not only marks *Minecraft* out from a lot of its competitors, it also allows participants to apply a lot of imagination to it—in a similar way that kids do with simple building toys like Lego.

Notch was a gaming enthusiast himself, so he didn't think like a product designer. He simply created something that he thought he and others like him might enjoy: "I designed the game for myself," he says. "That is an audience I know."

Notch released the prototype version of *Minecraft* on to a gaming forum in May 2009. From day one, he made two important decisions: first, he charged people to use the game, and second, he invited others to participate in *Minecraft*'s development. Fans were encouraged to come up with "mods"—modifications to the game that add to it or improve it in some way.

Notch started to blog about *Minecraft* and uploaded some videos on YouTube showing how it worked. Notch's approach was the antithesis of the pushy visionary. He did not try to force his will on the game—he allowed others to contribute to it and steer it in a way he had never imagined. In essence, what he was charging for was not a game, but access to an experimental workshop that allowed a group to show up and create something collaboratively. In many ways what he established was not dissimilar to the lab that George Merck set up for research scientists in New Jersey—except that it was online.

Minecraft wasn't designed top-down, it emerged from this group of developers and enthusiasts. By June 2010, it was robust enough to be released as an alpha version, and six months later

Notch was generating enough income to give up his day job and start a small company he called "Mojang" to support its development. "Mojang" means "gadget" in Swedish, a nod to Notch's developer roots.

Rather than basing Mojang in the business region of Stockholm like most other software companies, Notch based it in Södermalm, a once down-at-heel district (most famous for being the area that Stieg Larsson's *Girl with the Dragon Tattoo* was set in) that was being organically regenerated by hipsters and enthusiasts in a similar way to the Valley in Brisbane. It was an area that very much matched the ethos of Mojang and *Minecraft*.

Minecraft was communally developed through a beta phase and was released as a full-blown product in June 2011. There was no big-bang launch; its fan base grew retrovirally as one fan shared with the next through online gaming communities and enthusiast magazines.

By the end of the 2012, just three years after its conception and a little over a year after its "official" launch, *Minecraft* had 25 million registered participants and had generated $240 million in revenue.

A year later, the participant base had increased by 50 percent and was adding more than 20,000 new users every day. That is pretty good for a small independent company with fewer than 30 developers.

For those who participate in it, *Minecraft* is a deadly serious pursuit—something they engage in far more seriously than many people approach the jobs they are paid to do. It encourages mass collaboration, with huge groups working on all sorts of fiendishly complex projects together. The attention to detail in some of its structures is staggering. It also attracts fans from all ages and walks of life—from seven-year-old kids to groups of serious academics.

When I ask Lisa what it is about *Minecraft* that particularly attracts her, she frowns for a moment, then gestures at the shop.

"Because this is what I have on offer," she says. "I'm grateful to have the opportunity to travel to Australia, but all I can do for work is this or work in a coffee shop or on the fruit farms. I get offered jobs in massage shops. To Australians, I am just another Asian girl… And back home, I have to work for a big company, at my desk all day… But with *Minecraft*, I can be myself. I can use my creative skills. I can work on something I care about with others."

This juxtaposition of fellowship and personal endeavour lies at the heart of its attraction—Lisa feels part of and accepted by a community with whom she has a strong sense of affinity, while at the same time she is empowered and challenged to achieve things individually that she is personally proud of.

In gaming language, this is called "coopetition" (pronounced co-opetition)—an environment that is collaborative and competitive in equal measure. To participants, it manifests as a game—but a game that everyone takes very seriously indeed. Coopetitive—or collaboratively competitive—cultures underpin how communities of fans and enthusiasts work.

Traditionally, workplaces tend to be either competitive and high-performing, but have the kind of cultures that fill our bodies with angry and toxic stress hormones, or they are supportive and collaborative, but get bogged down in process, risk aversion, and group-think.

Collaboratively competitive cultures provide the best of both. Sports fans love to feel part of a tribe, but also to continually compete with each other on who knows most and who went to which game. Music fans are the same—they share their knowledge and downloads, but are competitive when it comes to who knows what and has the rarest limited editions. Instagram was all about sharing, but it is also about how many likes you get and the quality of your comments. The labs at Merck had a culture that encouraged scientists to experiment, share, and play, but also to continually strive to discover new and better ways to alleviate human suffering. It is in this juxtaposition that we feel most supported and alive.

Minecraft's influence had gone way beyond the online world. MinecraftEdu, a partnership set up by enthusiasts in Spain, Finland, and New York City, helps teachers use *Minecraft* as a virtual classroom for everything from maths to art and design. Schools in other countries are beginning to use *Minecraft* as a way to help students develop design and collaboration skills. Parents, realising the positive effect it has on their children, are beginning to rethink their views on gaming as a good/bad use of time.

Universities and business schools are seeing their model challenged by online educational offerings like the Khan Academy and massive open online courses, or MOOCs.

Minecraft shows how participatory innovation can be used not just to bring education online, but to engage people in a whole different way of learning—through group participation rather than individual study; learning through doing together, rather than learning alone, then doing.

It also points to how the principles of participatory innovation can make a difference in society. As mentioned earlier, in the London borough of Newham, one of the poorest areas in the UK, state-funded schools that would traditionally be at the bottom of the national educational performance tables are performing well above the national average by developing collaboratively competitive cultures that balance putting an onus on maintaining safe inclusive cultures with a rigorous focus on personal achievement and growth. A similar level of success is being seen in California's San Quentin State Prison, where inmates who have been through the participatory "Code.7370" coding schools have a 50 percent lower rate of re-offending when they leave prison – primarily because they have a means to find meaningful employment. And we saw earlier how Homeboys Industries, a social enterprise founded in Los Angeles by a Jesuit priest named Greg Boyle, has a high success rate in rehabilitating gang members, and how it achieves this by putting a focus on how to help them participate in society. Again, this is done by combining a focus on creating a safe social culture that people feel part of with an onus on developing both the social and technical skills needed to get into the workplace (this includes more than 800 free tattoo removal sessions a month, provided free by volunteer doctors). "Nothing stops a bullet like a job," says Father Boyle, neatly summing up Homeboys' social mission.

In September 2012, the United Nations Settlements Program announced the launch of "block by block", an initiative designed to encourage people to re-imagine 300 run-down public spaces across the globe using *Minecraft*; its first area of focus being the Kibera slum in Nairobi, Kenya. This project is something that Lisa is particularly interested in. She was trained as a designer in Taipei but wasn't able to find any meaningful work. The UN initiative has suggested a means for her and her friends to start to use *Minecraft* to develop and pitch ideas for urban renewal back in Taiwan—something her network of *Minecraft* co-creators had started to explore.

In October 2013, *Minecraft* received what might be the ultimate accolade. It was affectionately parodied in the American TV programme *South Park*. The show's Corey Lanskin character summed it up thus: "*Minecraft*, it don't got no winner. It don't got no objective. You just fuckin' build an' shit."

Like many a good joke, this gets to the essence of what

Minecraft is about far better than any wordy academic analysis.

What *Minecraft* shows is that we are entering an era when the concept of "ownership" is shifting—from something that implies physical or legal ownership to one that is about an emotional bond and a desire to be part of something and contribute.

The whole concept of a "consumer society" is being subverted. Young people like Lisa don't want to consume, they want to connect: to collaborate, to be involved, to create and participate—to "build an' shit".

The game is the organising model of the new social economy. But not just any old game—the deadly serious game—a game that feels deadly serious to those involved. It is coopetitive, meaning that it is both collaborative and competitive. It is networked. And it builds from the bottom up.

The organisational model that has for so long characterised our society—whether in the form of democracy, autocracy or corporations—is the hierarchy, a pyramidal structure in which the power lies at the top and is applied top down.

The deadly serious game lies at the heart of iTunes and Apple's App Store. It is the organising model of Facebook, Instagram, and YouTube. It is the mechanism that creates the dynamic energy of eBay, Uber, and Airbnb. It drives the explosive growth of participatory activities like yoga and road cycling. It is the system that is driving the high-growth businesses in the new economy—from enterprise start-ups, to fintech, to education, to healthcare.

On 15 September 2014, Microsoft bought Mojang for $2.5 billion. At the time of the acquisition, Notch Persson owned 71 percent of its shares.

10. How to be a billionaire in three easy moves: part 3

"What is real? How do you define 'real'? If you're talking about what you can feel, what you can smell, what you can taste and see, then 'real' is simply electrical signals interpreted by your brain"

Morpheus, *The Matrix*

The long white beaches that run down the coast just south of the Borobudur temple in Java, where I hung out with Putri and her friends, have the most fantastic surf. The giant waves roll down to the southeastern tip of the island, an area surfers know as "G-Land", where long waves regarded by many as the most ridable in the world seem to barrel in forever. The point break on the east side of Grajagan Bay is generally regarded as the best left-hand wave there is.

Just across the narrow strip of water that separates Java from Bali, the stunning beaches and epic surf continue down the south side of the latter island, eventually losing their sheen as the coastal strip builds up into what becomes the over-developed tourist sprawl that is Kuta.

This is the coastline where Nick Woodman developed GoPro.

The beaches are studded with surf schools, and just inland, yoga resorts.

I touched on the story of GoPro in the Introduction, but it is worth taking a closer look. Not only is it a great example of how to build a successful participatory business in the emerging new economy, it also a reveals a critical insight into what makes some digital products so spectacularly successful. I'll flag up now that it is a potential "Galileo moment", as it challenges some fundamental notions of what constitutes "good design".

Woodman's motivation was similar to that of George Eastman at Kodak and Edwin Land at Polaroid—he had no interest in technology *per se* and was not interested in "disrupting an industry". What he was interested in was how he might develop a better and more intimate way to capture and share his experience of surfing with his friends and peers.

As mentioned earlier, his first experiments were far from satisfactory, yet he pressed on, with additional feedback and support from fellow surf enthusiasts who played their part in his serious game.

His next idea was to mount a 35mm film camera on a belt. This worked better, good enough for others to be interested in buying it. He sold his first official "product" in 2004.

This "heuristic"—or trial-and-error—approach to product development is a critical characteristic of the participatory innovation mind-set. There was no hanging out in labs trying to develop the perfect product. Woodman's lab was the waves, and his cohorts were the other surfers who clustered around him in the café as he shared his early results. It was an agile, iterative process. Like Eastman's trip to the Dominican Republic and Land's moment on the beach with his daughter, Woodman's insight emerged directly from real-life experience. There was no need for focus groups or workshops on what users might need—like Simon Mottram at Rapha, Woodman had deep empathy with the needs of the user, because he *was* the user.

In his first year, he sold $150,000 worth of wrist-mounted 35mm video cameras—not a bad start at all.

But it was two years later that things really began to take off, when GoPro introduced its first "Hero" digital camera, and at the same time launched software that allowed GoPro clips to be easily shared and viewed online. Revenue jumped to $800,000. The following year, it quadrupled to $3.4 million.

And this is where it is worth taking a beat. Because this is where the true genius of Woodman's participatory innovation really began to show up.

Twenty years before Woodman had the quarter-life crisis that led him to the beaches of Bali, Giacomo Rizzolatti, a neuroscientist at the University of Parma in Italy, was working in a lab with a group of his students. What Rizzolatti and his team were interested in was the "premotor cortex," an area of the brain known to be instrumental in the planning and initiation of movement. To help them understand how the premotor cortex worked, they had rigged up an experiment to monitor the electrical activity in the brain of a macaque monkey.

The experiment consisted of getting the monkey to perform a series of manual tasks while Rizzolatti and his students monitored which neurons fired in the premotor cortex, helping them to build a picture of specifically which neurons were responsible for initiating and controlling which movement. The experiment was going pretty much as they had planned until they decided to take lunch—and this is where they made a discovery that gets right to the heart of why Woodman's innovation was so spectacularly successful.

If Rizzolatti's team had been based in northern Europe, what they stumbled across might never have happened. Instead of grabbing a sandwich at their desks, Rizzolatti took the team out for a leisurely lunch, Italian-style. When they returned, one of the students was eating an ice cream he'd bought. As he passed in front of the monkey, one of his colleagues noticed something strange: the monitors registered that the monkey's premotor cortex had come to life, even though the monkey hadn't moved. He asked his colleague with the ice cream to move back in front of the monkey while eating it and the same thing happened.

What Rizzolatti's team had discovered are what he later called "mirror neurons", neurons that fire when we observe someone else doing a task in exactly the same way as if we were undertaking the task ourselves.

It took a while for Rizzolatti's findings to be taken seriously because they seemed so strange even to him. As he said in an interview in the *New York Times* in 2006: "It took us several years to believe what we were seeing." He published a short piece on his findings a year after the experiment, but no one really paid any attention. It wasn't until four years later, when he published a far more detailed account in *Brain Magazine*, that the implications of what his team had discovered really landed, triggering a surge of research—over the following 10 years, more than 300 papers were published on different aspects of how mirror neurons work.

Mirror neurons begin to explain a lot of what can seem like very strange human behaviour—from why we get quite so obsessed and immersed in watching sports to why pornography is so addictive to some people. As far as the brain is concerned, when mirror neurons are firing it is exactly the same as if the body itself was involved.

On 13 May 2012, Manchester United's arch rivals, Manchester City, played Queens Park Rangers in the final game of the English Premier League season. Man City had to win the match to guarantee their first league title in more than 40 years. With the match four minutes into overtime and the scores equal, Man City's Argentinian striker, Sergio Agüero, broke through the defence and slotted the ball into the core of the net with a sublime strike. The crowd went wild, and Agüero, knowing Man City had won, broke the rules of the game and stripped off his shirt, waving it ecstatically above his head as he ran over to celebrate in front of Man City's fans.

As the TVs cameras panned across the crowd, it picked out a comical sight. A number of Man City's fans had followed suit and were mimicking Agüero's action. The men in question were probably around the same age as Agüero, but unlike him they were not in great shape. They looked highly uncomfortable doing what they were doing—as if they weren't quite sure why they were doing it. This was mirror neurons at work.

One of the reasons sports fans get so caught up in the game, so passionate and angry, is because as far as their brains are concerned they are participating. Their mirror neurons are firing and they are having the experience of being in the game. The ending of the Man City game was so explosive that some fans actually acted out what their brains were experiencing.

Mirror neurons explain why the combination of GoPro's "point-of-view" camera and easy-to-use software was so successful—GoPro didn't just allow those involved in extreme pursuits to participate more fully, it allowed the brains of those viewing it to have the experience of participating too. In an industry sector dominated by electrical giants, and with digital video cameras, seemingly in every shape, size, and price bracket, already available, the retroviral network effect kicked in. GoPro videos started to clock up millions of views on YouTube, and as they did, surfers and mountain bikers started to rethink what they might do for those who now had the experience of travelling with them rather than watching from a distance—it became about sharing the rush, not the spectacle.

They also explain why Instagram's low-res strategy and Notch Persson's rudimentary graphical approach were so successful. Commercial designers have a habit of wanting to design highly stylised products and experiences, giving our brains no place to participate. Instagram's suggestively grainy images and *Minecraft*'s simple characters allow the mirror neurons to connect with the essence of the experience, and then the brain fills in the rest. Less is so much more to a hungry brain. It doesn't want to watch, it wants to take part.

This requires a shift in design thinking.

There is a myth that Apple designs perfect products, but they intentionally don't. A new iPhone might look sleek and elegant in the shop, but it isn't designed for the real world. It is like a car with no fenders or seatbelts. It needs screen protection and a case if it is going to last more than two days in an average person's life. Leaving the product unfinished is a great way to encourage people to pay for add-ons, but, more importantly, it provides the opportunity for the user's brain to get involved, customising and modifying and figuring out what will work best.

The genius of Woodman's innovation wasn't just that it allowed surfers and other extreme-sports fans the means to participate more fully in what they were passionate about—it enabled those who viewed the videos to experience participating too, their mirror neurons firing as they leaned forward and immersed themselves on their computer or mobile screens.

GoPros started to show up wherever live action was happening. Shaun White, supercool pro skateboarder and Olympic snowboard champion, used a GoPro to capture his runs during the Winter X Games. The Rolling Stones deployed them onstage. The NFL tested embedding them in goal posts to capture touchdowns. Film directors Danny Boyle and Michael Bay experimented with them in their movies. Even the police and US military got on board—using them to create real-world scenarios in training exercises. GoPro shifted the relationship between the viewer and the content from "watching" to "experiencing".

Just 10 years after Woodman was paddling into the surf in Bali with a plastic bag on his hand, a quarter of all digital video cameras sold in the United States were GoPro Heroes. At the same time, GoPro videos were racking up tens of millions of views on YouTube. When Austrian skydiver Felix Baumgartner stepped from the platform of a hot-air balloon 24 miles above the earth's surface to break the world free-fall record, he had GoPros attached to his feet, hands, and helmet—completely redefining the meaning of "a lean-forward experience". Meanwhile, down on *terra firma*, when a New York City firefighter used a GoPro to capture and share his experience of saving a kitten from a tree, the video clocked up more than 20 million views in just a few days (begging the interesting question as to how many views Baumgartner might have got if he'd jumped with a kitten).

Woodman became a billionaire when GoPro went public, valued at almost $3 billion, but he still looks, sounds, and acts like a surf fan—albeit one with a love of flying Gulfstream jets. He's still a man who likes to show off and let others know about it. He still knows why he does what he does and ensures the rest of his company knows it. Like Kodak and Polaroid, GoPro's challenge, especially should Woodman ever step down, is not to forget that. They are not in the business of video cameras or digital content; they are in the business of human connection.

11. A higher calling

"For a hundred years now, we've been singing war songs about addicts. I think all along, we should have been singing love songs to them. Because the opposite of addiction is not sobriety, the opposite of addiction is connection"

Johann Hari,
Chasing the Scream: The First and Last Days of the War on Drugs

As we swing off the interstate into Palm Canyon Drive, John finally relaxes. He has been distractedly tapping the steering wheel all the way from Los Angeles.

We head into the canyon and the sun starts to dance along the ridge of the high wall. Long shadows jag across the road, and suddenly the air seems a lot cooler.

John dangles his arm down the side of the open-top Mustang and allows himself a smile.

"OK, then," he says, the flaring sunlight glinting on his aviators as he turns and grins at me. "Let's do this."

By the time we turn into the outskirts of Palm Springs, the sun has disappeared behind the canyon wall, lending the city a beautiful, dreamy glamour—the tousled tops of the high palm trees backlit and stark, the rest of the town sinking into a soft purple haze.

Palm Springs first became fashionable in the early 1900s, when rich Californians attracted to the light and clean air started to hang out there. But it wasn't until the 1930s, when studio-tied stars from the burgeoning Hollywood movie industry took a shine to it, that it really took off. The city was close enough to LA for stars to fulfil their contractual obligation to be on call, while being far enough away from the prying eyes of the press to get up to all sorts of capers that their contracts, keen to portray them as squeaky-clean members of society, forbade. Palm Springs has been associated with glamour and debauchery ever since. It's why young men like the one we are here to track down are drawn here—there is something epic and alluring about the place.

Like all rich areas, it needs a place for its itinerants and low-paid workers, and that is the neighbourhood we head into. Not seedy, just a little shabby and low-rent. We snake through some back streets and eventually pull up outside some kind of community hall. A group of men are standing outside in the gloom.

"There he is," John says. He pulls up the car and jumps out. "Stay here."

I watch as John approaches the group and a young man peels away from them. He's dressed in a baggy hoody and jeans, stooping slightly and smoking a cigarette. John talks to him for a moment, pats him on the arm...and then they hug. I feel awkward and touched in equal measure as I watch as the young man is visibly moved. They talk for a moment, then John returns to the car while the young man goes inside.

"Well, he's not dead," John says, with a grin. "Which is a start."

Ben is 22 years old and from Santa Monica, which is from where John knows him. He had been clean and sober for three months but has just relapsed, which is why we are here. Ben called John in the morning, and John told him to get to a meeting of Alcoholics Anonymous and that he'd meet him there.

John has had a roster of young men like Ben for 15 years now. At any one time, he has four or five with whom he is in regular contact. He told me as we drove out of town that this is the second time in the past two weeks that he has had to come to find Ben.

"Addiction's such a cunning, baffling, and powerful thing," he says, shaking his head. "Just when you think someone's got it beat, it rears up and bites them in the ass."

What John isn't, though, is a drug and alcohol addiction professional. He is not being paid to be here.

John is a 52-year-old executive in the movie industry. He is tanned, fit, and looks every bit the successful movie exec—a big smile, hearty handshake, bright-coloured Ralph Lauren polo shirt, and, of course, the beautiful dark-blue '60s Ford Mustang.

The reason John is here is because he is also a member of Alcoholics Anonymous.

Alcoholics Anonymous, or AA as it's known to its members, might not at first glance seem like a particularly interesting organisation. It is, as John puts it, "an organisation set up by a bunch of drunks and losers and run by a bunch of drunks and losers."

But that is what makes it so interesting. Because AA is not just an organisation run by a bunch of drunks and losers, it is an *extremely successful* organisation run by a bunch of drunks and losers. One that by many modern standards really shouldn't work.

AA has more than three million active members but no

overarching leadership structure. It is run bottom-up by a huge, loose network of members, all of whom at some point have been hopeless drunks. It doesn't employ any executives, managers, doctors, experts in addiction, or other professionals. The only thing that binds it together is its social mission. What AA calls its 'primary purpose'.

Everything AA does seems to fly in the face of "good practice". It goes out of its way to give jobs to people with no track record in doing them, often intentionally giving them to people with a track record in being really bad at them. If you are terrible with money, and even if you have stolen money, they will make you a treasurer. If you are disorganised and totally incapable of running your life, they will put you in charge of a meeting. If you are grumpy and really bad with people, they will give you the job of greeting people at the door.

Yet if it is measured by some of the key performance indicators of, say, a large healthcare provider, its impact is unparalleled.

AA is a multinational organisation, with operations in 170 countries. The average life span of a multinational corporation is 50 years. AA has now been operating over half as long again and shows no signs of flagging.

AA doesn't charge any fees for its services and takes no outside donations, yet it has been financially self-sufficient for well over half a century, steering its way through a world war and a number of severe economic downturns with no problems. It has never needed to reposition, restructure, or bring in turnaround consultants.

And most importantly, AA has a very successful product—one that works for people where all other methods have failed. What is more, it gives it away for free. It's like the Skype of addiction treatments.

AA—and its system of recovery, the 12-step programme (which has been appropriated by many other recovery programmes)—is the biggest and one of the most effective health-care systems on the planet. And it does it with no contributions from the public purse. In an era when health-care costs are soaring, and governments are struggling to balance the needs of aging and ever more demanding populations with reducing cost, there is much to be learned from AA.

The first group of what would come to be known as Alcoholics Anonymous was established in 1935 in Akron, Ohio, by two men, Bill Wilson and Bob Smith, who had both been written off as hopeless drunks. The organisation started in a way that is now familiar—as an informal gathering of people with a shared common purpose. What was different, though, was that rather than having a shared passion they were excited about, they shared a big problem: they were hopelessly and seemingly untreatable drunks.

The reason they had met was because Wilson had attended a Christian group called "the Oxford Group" and found that applying its principles to his alcoholism helped him get and stay sober. He shared this with Smith, another lost cause, who then also got sober. Wilson and Smith shared what they had with a small group of others. In the same way that successful institutions emerged out of the small groups at Lloyd's and Jonathan's coffee houses, AA grew out of that original gathering in Akron.

It is perhaps no surprise that Wilson was a prodigious coffee drinker. Those early meetings were usually over a coffee, and, back in those days, a cigarette. They were informal, passionate, and based on their common shared need—to get and stay sober.

The AA model didn't evolve by random chance, though. Wilson's approach was based on what he experienced at the Oxford Group, and that was based on a 2,000-year-old philosophy. He took the religion out of it but kept the underlying structure of how the Oxford Group operated. And the Oxford Group was based on a model that has its roots in ancient Greece.

This model is called a "koinonia", a Greek word that doesn't have a simple English translation, but is described by a set of characteristics, a number of which are already familiar to us. *Koinonia* are groups brought together and organised around a single, common purpose. In their Christian form, this was the desire to worship God, but with AA, it was the treatment of alcoholism. They are affiliations, based on a deep sense of belonging and ownership for everyone involved. They are networks, organised from the bottom up. They are based on the principles of intimacy, fellowship, shared experience, contribution, and participation. If we take God or alcoholism out of the equation and replace it with "road cycling", we could well be describing Rapha.

AA is an organisation with a clear social mission. Every AA meeting starts with the line "Our primary purpose is to stay sober and help other alcoholics to achieve sobriety," and that is all they focus on. They won't and don't get involved in anything else.

The organisation has no formal structure. It is a network that spread out from that original meeting—alcoholic to alcoholic passing it on. The same network effect we saw with Arctic Monkeys, an altruistic social retrovirus that has become an intrinsic part of the lives of those involved. Today, in addition to its more than three million active members, AA has many millions more in the medical, therapeutic, and faith-based organisations that interact with it.

When I asked John why he was prepared to leave work early

and cancel dinner with his girlfriend to chase down Ben, he laughed: "The only reason I go to AA is to stay sober and help other alcoholics to achieve sobriety. It's that simple, so here I am."

This sense of connection—to a higher purpose, to something that is meaningful and matters, and to a group of people with the same aim—is the invisible power that drives the extraordinary performance of organisations like AA, Apple, and Rapha. It is what has fans of teams like Manchester United get so deeply involved with them. It is what compelled the scientists at Merck to cure river blindness.

And in the case of the recovering alcoholics in AA, it is what helps them get and stay sober.

The two closest words we have in modern English to the meaning of *koinonia* are a "cause" or a "movement". The combination of these two words is revealing—a cause is a fundamental source of action, and movement means momentum. *Koinonia* cause people to take action—to get involved and take part. That is what gives them so much energy.

Many years after the deaths of AA's founders, and with no management structure to hold them to account, John and millions of other AA members around the world like him work tirelessly to fulfil the organisation's primary purpose.

The seemingly haphazard nature of AA's structure is an important part of its strength. When a group of people have such a fundamental connection and alignment with an organisation's social mission, traditional "command-and-control" management systems are not only no longer needed, they get in the way. The lack of constraint empowers people to take initiative and act. This is why AA's seemingly captainless ship works so well.

AA provides a template for how both commercial and

non-for-profit organisations work in the emerging new social and economic paradigm. Purpose is the root cause of its performance. The deadly serious game is its organising model. It is about participation not products. And it is built on a strong sense of shared experience and belonging

It is exactly the same model that is driving the high growth commercial organisations that are emerging in the new economy.

When Simon Mottram established Rapha, he didn't focus the business on making nice, functional cycling clothes. He was about the *why* not the *what*. What he talked about was the "glory through suffering" of serious road cycling. *That* was the social mission of Rapha. When he set out to get his first round of funding, this phrase "glory through suffering", and a couple of compelling pictures, was just about all he had. But in it and from it he was able to paint a picture of what the business would look like quite simply as he meant it. It was authentic and clear. People know when something is real, and when it is, they are attracted to it.

As an expression, "glory through suffering" might just sound like a catchy slogan. We've all become so used to being bombarded with slogans and advertising it is easy to shrug this off as marketing fluff.

The difference is that Rapha lives by it. It calls out to a certain kind of person: those who see the struggle and challenge of hard-core road cycling as a heroic endeavour. It gives them a deep sense of meaning and purpose.

When I visited Rapha's offices, I didn't find an office of designers and marketers trying to figure out how to evoke feelings consistent with a slogan. I found a bunch of road cycling enthusiasts totally committed to a cause who didn't look that different from the people in their café. As I walked around, listened to conversations, looked at what was on the wall, it was clear they weren't there just to make nice cycling tops, they were in the business of generating ways for people to experience the pain, sweat, and heroism of attacking the steep slopes of the High Alps and Pyrenees.

Manchester United are not just a football team. For their fans, they are a cause—they are a team that has risen against the odds from the gritty industrial north of England, with an "us-against-the-world" mentality. As far as they are concerned, they are the swaggering working-class underdogs, and play like their lives depend on it, even now they are the biggest sports franchise on the planet, full of highly paid overseas players. For Rapha and its fans, the game is the glory and suffering of road cycling. With AA it is showing that alcoholics who have been previously written off by everyone else can get and stay sober. What they all have in common is that their primary purpose is the fulfilment of a social mission. A big why. They are out to prove a point.

In 2011, Martin Shkreli, a 28-year-old New Yorker who had made a fortune as a hedge fund manager, bought a pharmaceutical company called Retrophin. The company owned the rights to Thiola, a drug used by 20,000 patients in the United States to treat rare and incurable kidney diseases. One of the first things Shkreli did was bump up the price of Thiola from $2 to $42—his instinct as a hedge fund manager was to look at how to maximise the return on his investment.

Four years later, Shkreli started a company called Turing Pharmaceuticals and acquired the rights to Daraprim, a drug used to treat HIV and malaria. Shortly after acquiring Daraprim, Shkreli announced he was hiking the price of the medication from $25 to an incredible $1,050. The pill cost about $1 to make.

The media caught hold of the story. Shkreli appeared on TV to try to explain the price hike, but his carefully constructed words—which may well have impressed fellow investors—set the millennial bullshit detector off like a klaxon. Shkreli was slaughtered in social media, and did a vague attempt at a backdown.

But the damage was done. Turing Pharmaceuticals showed just how far the pharmaceutical industry had strayed from George Merck's founding social purpose.

AA shows how participatory innovation can be used to create a different healthcare model—one that is run by and for those involved, and no one else.

There is a dynamic collaborative competition to participation in AA. It is a deadly serious game. Everyone is in it together, and people like John will bend over backwards to help other members out. But there is also a keen focus on personal recovery and growth. John can tell you with great pride exactly how many years and days he is sober.

With healthcare costs steadily rising, and public health care under mounting pressure, participatory innovation provides the possibility of a whole different model, shifting from one in which patients act as consumers, tying to extract services from an increasingly stretched resource, to one in which everyone is involved.

Three months after I'd been to Palm Springs, I gave John a call. That night had left an indelible print in my memory. There had been something deeply moving about hanging out with John and Ben, seeing the difference John's turning up had made, and just how committed he was to Ben.

John was in good cheer when we spoke, which didn't surprise me—he was like that all the time we were together, even when he was talking about or dealing with some very serious stuff.

John told me Ben had managed to get a couple of weeks up sober after we had met but then had relapsed again. Finally, though, he seemed to be getting things together.

"Do you think he'll make it?" I ask hopefully.

John laughs.

"Who knows?" he says. "Some do, some don't. My job is just to help out as best I can."

"Isn't it frustrating?" I ask.

"Completely!" he says.

"Then why do you do it?"

"Why?" He pauses. "When you come into AA, they tell you sponsoring someone will be the best thing you can do, that you'll get much more out of it than you put into it. I always thought that sounded hokey. Like some bullshit excuse to get you to do good. But you know what? They were right. I've had the privilege of doing some pretty cool stuff in my work. But none of it compares to the satisfaction I get out of this. Really. If I can help one human being stay sober, it feels like I have done something really worthwhile. That my life has some sort of higher purpose, and that is pretty awesome."

12. It ain't what you do, it's the why that you do it

"Everybody loves something, even if it's just tortillas"

Chögyam Trungpa, Tibetan Buddhist master

In 1938, the Academy of Motion Picture Arts and Sciences hosted its 10th annual award ceremony in Hollywood, an event that had come to represent everything that was glamorous and glitzy about the industry that had been enabled by George Eastman's great invention.

The awards had unofficially become known as the Oscars. Being Hollywood, many people claimed to have invented the term, but like most slang no one really knew the source—Betty Davis's suggestion that it was because she had named hers after her first husband, Harmon Oscar Nelson, was perhaps the most charming.

All the stars showed up, pictures of rude health, great teeth, and happy relationships. This was the public face of Hollywood; anything that didn't fit with the all-American dream left firmly behind in Palm Springs.

The Oscar for Best Actor in a Leading Role went to Spencer

Tracey, for his portrayal of Father Flanagan in the movie *Boys Town*. The award for Best Actor in a Supporting Role went to Walter Brennan, like Tracey an actor of Irish-American descent, for his role in the movie *Kentucky*.

Now if you are a movie buff, you may well know Walter Brennan. He is regarded by many critics as one of the finest character actors there has ever been, playing gritty, real roles in just about every genre.

But if you are not a movie buff, then chances are you have never heard of him. Tracey, however, remains one of the legendary names of the great Hollywood era.

This is the way it goes with awards: we remember the winners of the most prestigious awards, but the rest tend to pass us by. Brennan is one of only three men to have won three Oscars for acting, but as his were for supporting roles, few people recall him. The other two—leading men Jack Nicholson and Daniel Day-Lewis—are household names.

Now imagine if there were an annual Oscar ceremony for iconic American products. There'd be many high-profile contenders for Best Leading Product—Levi's jeans, Kodak film, and the iPhone would all at various times have been in with a shout. Much as they are now out of fashion, Lucky Strike cigarettes might have won back in 1938.

The list wouldn't ever include the humble Californian tomato.

But if there were an Oscar for Best Supporting Product, the Californian tomato would be a multiple winner. It plays a critical role in baked beans, Heinz ketchup, and McDonald's burgers. It is the key ingredient in Campbell's tomato soup, and, by association, Andy Warhol's pop art. And, of course, it is vital to salsa, and pizza and pasta sauce—ubiquitous products Americans have made their own. The Californian tomato is the Walter Brennan of American products—hugely important and highly successful, but never centre-stage. Thus it tends just to get overlooked.

It is therefore perhaps not surprising that one of the most extraordinary companies most people have never heard of is in the business of Californian tomatoes.

Morning Star was set up as a three-truck tomato haulage business in 1970, joining the never-ending procession of tomato-laden vehicles that shuttle up and down I-80 outside Sacramento, California. Since then, it has grown at a double-digit clip for best part of 40 years, turning itself from a small trucking business into the world's largest and most successful tomato processor. Morning Star handles around 30 percent of all tomatoes processed in the United States every year. It processes, it cans, it delivers. If there is something to be done with a tomato, Morning Star is doing it.

As a business, Morning Star's performance has been genuinely extraordinary—four decades of double-digit growth in an industry that has an average of one percent growth a year.

But what makes Morning Star really extraordinary is that it has done all this with no management structure. Morning Star has no managers, no departments, and no chains of command. It is run bottom up by its employees, with no hierarchy or command and control above them. Everyone in the organisation is free and empowered to make decisions, including spending money. And no one reports to anyone.

Now applying traditional management thinking, or what for many people might just seem like common sense, this should be a recipe for disaster—if a fitter in a plant wants to order some new expensive gadget, he or she can just go out and buy one. That is insane.

But it works. Not only does it work, it has created a company that has consistently outperformed its rivals by an order of 10, and not just for a few years, but for decades. It is also not a small company or a simple business. It is integrated, complex, and capital-intensive.

What Morning Star shows is that you don't need a serious or worthy issue to deal with to create a cause.

Morning Star is organised around one clear defining purpose: "to produce tomato products and services which consistently achieve the quality and service expectations of our customers…"

Now clear as this is, it's fair to say that sexy it is not. No disrespect to Morning Star, but this is not the kind of inspirational line that people will be posting on Facebook alongside quotes from Steve Jobs, Albert Einstein, and Gandhi. And it doesn't have the noble calling that a cause like Alcoholics Anonymous has.

They are just tomatoes, for God's sake!

But for Morning Star colleagues, this is a heroic endeavour—one they participate in with an incredible amount of passion, intensity, and commitment.

A visit to the company's processing plant in Los Banos, in the heart of California's tomato country, is an unsettling experience. It really isn't clear who is in charge. People doing the kind of jobs where you might normally expect them to just stick to a job description or wait to be told what to do are highly active and engaged in looking at how to improve how things work. The people who work for Morning Star aren't called staff or employees, they are called colleagues, and this isn't just some faddy management term—they really act like colleagues.

Morning Star shows how participatory innovation can be applied to any business, and the impact it has on morale, performance and results.

The only structure the company uses is a contract each colleague draws up every year called a "Colleague Letter of Understanding". What this boils down to is a personal statement of how the individual will contribute to fulfilling the company's purpose, and how he or she will contribute directly to the colleagues they interact with. This is then reviewed horizontally by those the commitments are aimed at, and it is tuned, negotiated and tightened until everyone is happy. The result is a network of interlocking agreements that, together, are all focused on making the business work. Beyond that, colleagues are just left to get on with it. There's no fulfilling a role or working inside a function—the only thing that matters is delivering on specific agreed outcomes.

This process unlocks the inherent creativity, ingenuity, and commitment of everyone who works there. It encourages them to build relationships based on mutual trust and commitment, rather than simply complete tasks. Everything everyone does every day is in service of producing "tomato products and services which consistently achieve the quality and service expectations of our customers." That's it!

The paradox of Morning Star is that it is the lack of management and control that allows the colleagues to build a highly resilient and flexible structure that gives the company the optimum means to succeed. It is fast, flexible, and highly innovative.

And given that middle management can account for up to 35 percent of a large company's wages, it also means they are doing it in a particularly lean and cost-effective way.

Top-down hierarchical organisations tend to trap people in functions and silos, and focus them on job descriptions and tasks, especially as they grow larger. The mechanisms of management and reporting often become more important than the job itself. People get caught up in internal machinations, politics, and faffing around with email. By removing all constraints and distractions, those who work for networked organisations like Morning Star and AA are left liberated and empowered to focus simply on the only reason they are there: the fulfilment of the organisation's purpose.

Morning Star shows that what you do doesn't have to be virtuous or glamorous to become a cause. The colleagues of Morning Star work with all the same passion, commitment and verve as the members of AA, and the company's extraordinary performance and results reflect that.

But is Morning Star's seemingly crazy decentralised model scalable? Morning Star is a complex business, but it is still midsized and privately owned. Is it perhaps an anomaly, born out of freewheeling 1970s California? The principles of a *koinonia* work for a giant organisation like AA, where members have a deep and personal connection with the purpose of the organisation. But could this decentralised and de-layered approach really work in huge, complex, conservative commercial organisations, the kind of businesses where hierarchies and chains of command are seen as essential to the wellbeing of a successful enterprise?

Evidence from the other side of the world suggests it could. The Haier Group is one of China's most successful industrial conglomerates, based in Qingdao on the country's industrial east coast. Its transformation from a dysfunctional fridge maker in the mid-1980s to a white-goods powerhouse today mirrors the transformation of the country itself. In 2013, one in three of all appliances bought in China came from Haier. The company employs more than 70,000 people and has 24 manufacturing plants spread across the globe. It is by all measures an industrial giant, and one born out of China, a country famed for its top-down management and love of command and control.

In 2000, Haier was the first Chinese company to start

manufacturing in the United States, building a plant in South Carolina, but they failed to convince the American public that they were anything other than a maker of cheap, second-rate appliances, and never cracked more than five percent market share.

In 2009, Zhang Ruimin, Haier's CEO, decided dramatic action was needed. It was Zhang who has been the architect of Haier's original turnaround, famously taking a sledgehammer to one of the company's many faulty fridges, then urging employees to go through the warehouses and do the same to any fridges they found to be faulty or shoddily made. Zhang's sledgehammer is still on the wall in the corporate headquarters.

Zhang realised that if Haier wanted to be taken seriously in more developed markets, and go head-to-head with American market leader Whirlpool, it was going to have to radically shift the perception the public had of it. And to do that was going to take more than just window dressing—it needed to become a hothouse of innovation.

"As a company gets bigger, there is usually stricter control on its employees and less room for them to take ownership of their work," Zhang conceded. "This is a challenge both for Chinese companies and companies across the globe."

Zhang's solution was as radical as sledgehammering fridges in the 1980s. He didn't just tinker with the company's structure; he ripped it out, completely removing hierarchy, functions, and middle management, and structuring the company around what he called "self-managed teams". These teams are not quite as autonomous as Morning Star, they still have to gain approval for projects to go ahead, but rather than a stodgy risk-averse bureaucracy, Haier has a lean, agile process that rewards innovation and ideas. Any employee can have an idea and, if it is approved, can then set up an autonomous self-managed team. By 2012, there were 2,000 teams in the company, and the results were beginning to come on-stream. A team led by Lei Yongfeng, a veteran engineer liberated by the new culture, developed a new kind of air conditioning unit, something that has never been seen on the market before. When the unit, called the Tianzun, went on sale, it set a new record for the number of air-conditioning units sold in one day.

"We have become more and more entrepreneurial," said Lei, when asked what had changed. "We grab every opportunity, just as if it is our own business."

Morning Star and Haier employ exactly the same kind of decentralised organisational model as AA—one based on the principles of a *koinonia*. For it to work, those involved have to be galvanised around a strong sense of common commitment and purpose, something that occurs to them as important and heroic. Talking to the colleagues in Morning Star's plants and engineers in Haier's labs, you can hear the steely passion in their voices—there is an excitement and vigour in the room.

13. The pursuit of happiness

"Gross national product does not allow for the health of our children, the quality of their education or the joy of their play. It does not include the beauty of our poetry or the strength of our marriages, the intelligence of our public debate or the integrity of our public officials. It measures neither our wit nor our courage, neither our wisdom nor our learning, neither our compassion nor our devotion to our country. It measures everything, in short, except that which makes life worthwhile"

Robert F Kennedy

Happiness is a pretty poor measure of happiness. If you look at the countries that regularly come out on top in international happiness rankings, they also have high rates of suicide, divorce, alcoholism, and depression.

When I travelled from Jakarta to Seoul, what struck me when I arrived in Seoul was that it felt a lot less happy than Jakarta. Seoul is a sophisticated, modern, well-organised city; Jakarta, a gridlocked chaos where the drains overflow when it rains—and it rains a lot. Seoul is ranked 25 places higher than Jakarta in the United Nations Happiness Report. But in Seoul, people laughed less and they interacted less. For all its austere beauty, it seemed a city obsessed with cosmetic surgery. In Jakarta, there was a vibe, an energy, a deep sense of connection.

Every year, more than 30,000 people are killed in the United States with firearms—by far the highest number per head of any county that isn't a war zone. Given the high-profile media coverage that gun crime gets in the United States, this may not surprise you.

But what might surprise you is that more than 60 percent of those deaths are suicides; nearly twice as many Americans kill themselves with firearms than are killed by others.

This is just the tip of a humanitarian crisis.

As I mentioned earlier, more than 12 million people in the US regularly abuse and misuse opiates, with more than 40,000 people admitted to emergency rooms annually, following overdoses or mental breakdown. And levels of self-destructive behaviour, stress and distress are similar in the UK, while most Western countries are wracked by extraordinarily high divorce rates and people suffering from social isolation.

We live in increasingly socially dislocated times, and the human consequences are devastating.

A couple of months after his 66th birthday, Stamatis Moraitis, a Greek-American living in Florida, was diagnosed with lung cancer. His doctors told him that the disease was well advanced, but if they treated it aggressively he might get better. When he asked about his chances of recovery, he was given a 50-50 chance. Moraitis didn't like the odds, or what he would have to go through. He declined the treatment. He decided his time had come, and started to prepare for the end of his life.

Moraitis was originally from a small island off Greece called Ikaria, and had emigrated to America at the end of the Second World War, keen to build a new life. He ended up living in Florida, as the warm weather agreed with his Mediterranean genes. But now that he was looking death in the eye, he had a strong urge to return to where he was born.

Moraitis left America and returned home to Ikaria to see out his days. And that is what he did—for the next 36 years. On returning to Ikaria, Moraitis slowly regained his health, lived a happy life, and died in 2012 at the grand old age of 102.

Now if this was just a one-off, it could be passed off as one of those strange things that happens every so often—a freak of nature. But it is not. It is a particularly extreme example, but not out of the ordinary in Ikaria. There's something about Ikaria that seems to help people live longer and healthier lives. An Ikarian is two and half times more likely to reach 90 than an American, and on average they live 10 years longer than other Europeans.

This phenomenon has intrigued scientists for years, and the island is often visited by researchers. There are many possible contributing factors: good, simple food, clean air, a nice climate, a slow pace of life. But there are many other places in the world that have all these things where people don't live so long.

There are two very noticeable outstanding factors when you visit Ikaria. The first is that it is an extremely sociable place—social and laid-back in equal measure. People are in and out of one another's houses; they meet and talk in the squares. You are never alone on Ikaria. If you want to connect with people or sit down and chat, there is always someone available, but there is no pressure to do so.

The second is that older people remain active participants in society—there is no sitting around in old-people's homes. On Ikaria, Moraitis tended vines in an olive grove until the day he died. The concept of "retiring" just doesn't exist. Old people are included in the day-to-day lives of their families and have a vibrant social network. They hang out; they are involved. There's a sense that Ikaria is a project everyone is involved in.

Dr Clifford Saron is a research scientist at the Center for Mind and Brain at the University of California, Davis. In 2010, he led a team that set out to look into the physiological effects of meditation.

The team invited a group of men who regularly meditated to attend a three-month meditation retreat so they could monitor the physiological effects of meditating over time.

The research showed a profound physiological response. As the men mediated, they started to produce higher levels of an enzyme that builds telomeres. Telomeres are the protective caps that sit on the end of our chromosomes. Over time, as cells divide, telomeres diminish, a factor that triggers the aging process, and in some cases the onset of cancer. Higher levels of the enzyme arrest this process, and thus slow up the aging process and reduce the risk of cancer.

The most obvious conclusion to draw from the study was that the production of the enzyme was caused by meditation—that is, after all, what they set out to prove.

Fortunately, Dr Saron wasn't one of those scientists who just went looking for evidence to prove what he was out to prove. He was curious. There was another pattern in the data—a clear correlation between the hormone levels in each man and the significance he attributed to the practice: the more importance given to meditation, the greater the levels of hormone.

What Dr Saron began to conclude was that it wasn't the meditation per se that was making the difference, but how meaningful it was to those who practised it.

This was a great insight.

But it was actually only half the picture. The problem with a lot of data science and research is the frame. Dr Saron's research was focused on the individual. What it missed was that the men were meditating in a group.

So much research into addiction, illness, and depression misses this point. Why do people so often get well in rehab but relapse when they leave? Why do people get fit in gym and yoga classes but find it hard to maintain fitness when they are on their own? Why have so many breakthroughs been in coffee shops, informal start-up garages, and communal tech hubs?

What he missed was hidden in plain sight.

What he didn't notice was something that I experienced in all the communities I visited that were like Ikaria, all the companies and organisations that produced extraordinary results in one way or another, all the social enterprises where people reported a deep sense of satisfaction in what they did, despite often being paid little or nothing for it.

It was something I saw in the people who were passionate road cyclists, those who participated in yoga, the people in 12-step groups like AA. All the places where people reported a deep sense of purpose and satisfaction in what they were doing.

It is something you can only notice by being there, because it doesn't show up in a lot of the data; it shows up in the felt experience.

It wasn't just that the men were doing something that felt significant and meaningful to them. It was that they were doing it within a community of which they felt themselves to be a part.

They were connected to something that was meaningful and mattered to them, they were able to participate in practising it on a daily basis, *and* they were connected with a community of like-minded people.

When we feel connected to those around us, our body relaxes. We feel safe, at home. We can let down our guard.

The sympathetic nervous system that keeps us in a state of high alert finds balance.

Our parasympathetic nervous system, the system that works on healing and regeneration, takes over.

We feel better, we live longer, our susceptibility to cancer and other serious illness is dramatically reduced. We heal, we regenerate, we grow, our deeper energy flows.

When Moriatis went home, what he discovered was connection—deeply rooted authentic human connection. This was the source of his recovery.

14. Together

"To be isolated from your band, and, especially when young, to be isolated from your particular caretaker is fraught with the greatest danger. Can we wonder then that each animal is equipped with an instinctive disposition to avoid isolation and to maintain proximity?"

John Bowlby, developmental psychologist

Kunming in southwest China is a thriving city of three million people. It sits at the nexus of the trade routes to Vietnam, Myanmar and Laos, so it is an important regional commercial hub. It also has a strong manufacturing sector and is working hard to turn itself into a tourist destination. It's a city that very much represents 21st-century China—energetic, ambitious, and modernising fast. Young people in skinny jeans and big sunglasses browse the stores, seemingly constantly in touch with someone on their smartphones.

But by Chinese standards, in a country of over a billion people, with a concentration of frenetic activity along its eastern seaboard, Kunming is still a bit of a backwater. There are many cities with a greater claim to fame.

Given Kunming's relatively lowly status, it was a little

surprising that Apple decided to open an Apple Store there in 2012.

What was far more surprising is that it would choose to open 22 of them.

That is how it looked in 2012. If you walked around the commercial centre of Kunming, it seemed as if Apple had been taking a leaf out of Starbucks' expansion strategy. In one central mall, there was a flagship Apple Store, and just around the corner two more smaller ones—each with the trademark brightly lit interior, austere flat surfaces, happy, helpful staff in blue T-shirts, and, of course, being an Apple Store, lots of fans.

Was this some pilot for a new style of Apple blanket retailing in Asia?

It was difficult to tell. Apple's normally super-slick PR machine seemed to have caught a cold because if you visited the Apple website, there was no reference to Kunming. In fact, it only mentioned a few Apple Stores in China's major cities. It was quite hard to find out what they were up to.

The reason for this is that the stores hadn't actually been opened by Apple. They were what the Chinese call "shanzhai"— roughly translated, *shanzhai* means "rip-off". The stores were fake Apple Stores, counterfeits.

The news was broken by a young American woman named Jessica Angelson, who was working for an NGO in Kunming. Angelson stumbled on an Apple Store when she was walking around the city centre and was surprised to find two others nearby. The stores looked perfect at first sight, but on closer inspection she noticed they weren't quite right—there were some rough edges, some crucial details that were off. Then she found one that had a sign that said "Apple Stoer," and realised what was going on. Apple is famous for being fastidious about its brand, so while a few variations might have been allowed for a different market, there was no way a glaring misspelling would get through. She took pictures and shared them on her blog, which was soon picked up by the international press.

Apple's initial reaction was to assume Angelson had found resellers—the company had many in the area—and posted a list of addresses. But the stores Angelson had found weren't at those addresses. When Angelson went back to one of the stores, she found it had completely disappeared. A whole beautifully rendered Apple Store had just disappeared into thin air—a reaction to the international press getting wind of the story.

Building fake Apple Stores might seem like an audacious and slightly comical thing to do, but it actually points to what Simon Mottram was talking about in his presentation to the Luxury Brand Association in London.

Traditionally, Chinese people's primary and strongest affiliation has been with their family group. As the country has rapidly modernised and young people have flocked to huge anonymous cities like Kunming, this affiliation has started to break down. Suddenly, a whole generation has been left searching for its place in the world.

In 2009, Apple generated just two percent of its overall revenues from China; by 2012, it was up to 20 percent and rising sharply. This in a country where the price of an iPhone is twice the average monthly salary. There are many far cheaper alternatives available, many local ones with features the same as, or even better than, the iPhone. What young Chinese are paying for is way more than a smartphone.

Rapha was launched during a time of economic prosperity and optimism. Within just a few years, though, the global financial crisis hit and everything changed—the economies it operated in went into steep recession, and people's spending habits changed quickly. As a new business selling products that were both expensive and technically a "discretionary spend", you would expect this to have hit them hard.

It didn't though. In fact, the opposite happened. Rapha did what the legendary Italian road cyclist Marco Pantani did when he set the record for the fastest-ever accent of the dauntingly steep Alpe d'Huez in the 1997 Tour de France—seemingly defying logic by not only maintaining his pace, but actually getting faster as the hill got steeper. Rapha grew at a double-digit rate though the worst years of the Great Recession, at a time when all around it more established brands were struggling, and it has maintained a similarly blistering pace ever since. The factors behind this astonishing performance get right to the heart of why fans flock to Apple Stores—even fake ones—and why they are prepared to pay such high prices.

John Cacioppo, a professor in psychology at the University of Chicago, is an expert in the subject of social isolation. One of his areas of research has been the impact that social isolation has on the human body. What Cacioppo's studies have shown is that when people feel socially isolated, their bodies go into distress mode—triggering parts of the immune system that are responsible for wound healing and tackling bacterial infection. This is most likely in response to what the body perceives as a physical threat from being in a hostile environment; it readies itself to deal with attack and trauma. When this happens, it produces a hormone called "cortisol", a steroid designed to reduce swelling and inflammation. Cacioppo's research revealed that while high levels of stress hormones in the blood are OK for short periods, when the body remains in a constant state of "high alert" for long periods, persistently high levels of stress hormones (particularly cortisol) have a toxic effect. This accelerates the aging processes, and dramatically increases the risk of heart attack, dementia, cancer, depression and premature death.

We tend to associate social isolation with being physically isolated, but what makes the biggest difference is how we feel about where we are. A Dutch study published in the *Journal of Neurology, Neurosurgery & Psychiatry* in 2012 showed that older people who reported feeling lonely were more likely to develop dementia than others, regardless of how many friends they had or whether they lived alone. It was how connected they felt that made the difference. The research showed that feeling lonely was linked to a 64 percent increase in the risk of developing dementia. Age was obviously a contributing factor, but this research points to the long-term impact that being in environments we don't feel connected with has on our health and wellbeing.

"Social isolation is on a par with high blood pressure, obesity, lack of exercise, and smoking as a risk factor for illness and early death," said Cacioppo when he published his findings.

This is why affiliation is so important. It has a very profound effect on our brain chemistry and therefore our health. In situations where we feel a strong sense of affinity with those around us, our brains ramp down the production of stress hormones—this includes serotonin, a hormone designed to encourage us to stay on guard and in control. When our serotonin levels drop, our brains relax what is called the "ego boundary," the boundary it creates between ourselves and the outside world that gives us our sense of "self." In high-stress situations, the ego boundary is like a hard wall between our psyche and the outside world—creating a sense of "us and them", and a perception of the world as a hostile place. But in a situation where there is a strong sense of affinity, and serotonin levels drop, our ego boundary becomes far more porous. When this happens, instead of feeling isolated we start to feel connected to the world and those around us. In extreme cases, the ego boundary disappears completely—this is the sense of "merging" that we experience when we fall in love.

As the ego boundary relaxes, the brain also ups its production of dopamine, the "happy hormone". The purpose of this is to encourage us to do more of whatever we are doing. In this low-serotonin, high-dopamine state, we stop feeling anxious—as our body is not sending out distress signals and chemicals—and we experience a sense of serenity, affinity, and happiness.

Dopamine has another important effect beyond just making us feel high. It amplifies the brain's activity in certain parts of the cerebral cortex and closes down activity elsewhere. This has two effects: first, we become far more focused and thus effective at what we are doing; second, all the background noise and anxiety that so often distract us subside. The purpose of this "dopamine effect" is to help increase our chances of further success. When experienced in the extreme, this state is often referred to as "bliss" or "the zone".

The dopamine effect is critical both to the wellbeing of individuals who experience affiliation and also to the organisations to which they are affiliated. When the dopamine effect is at play, everyone wins.

Studies on human happiness routinely report facts that initially seem to make no sense. For example, low-income Filipino housekeepers in America are typically much happier than their rich employers. If we look for commonality across these studies, though, there is a common thread—the happiest people are those with a strong sense of affiliation to a group or community they feel part of and safe in. In the case of the Filipino housekeepers, they come from a society with a strong social network among women, and since there are a lot of poor Filipino immigrants in America, wherever they go there is a supportive network they can hook straight into. Their employees often live in gated communities cut off from the world, and work in competitive high-stress environments. The housekeepers experience the dopamine effect, their employees the toxic effects of high levels of cortisol and stress hormones lingering in their body.

In a time of an economic downturn, and against a backdrop of social change and global unrest, people feel more threatened and less looked-after by the society they live in. Hence the need to feel affiliation elsewhere becomes more pronounced. What this meant for Rapha is that what would otherwise have been seen as a "discretionary spend"—and thus the first to be cut in a tight economy—became an essential and subconscious investment in emotional wellbeing.

Most of the international press that covered the fake Apple Stores in Kunming focused their attentions on it being a sign of what they saw as China's flagrant disregard for intellectual property law—a valid point, although one that many Chinese resent, considering that so much of Apple's stuff is made in China.

But what they said less about was that this was also a great example of modern China's buccaneering entrepreneurialism. What the chancers who opened the *shanzhai* stores realised was that if you build an Apple Store, even a bad copy, fans will flock there. For young Chinese trying to find their place in the world, the Apple Store isn't just a shop. It is somewhere they identify with. Somewhere that mitigates the social isolation they feel in the new big cities. Something they feel part of, where they don't feel alone. Given the effects this has on their bodies, no wonder they show up.

15. Home

"We're not trying to create a shop, or an offer, or a set of products. It's an emporium. It's the sort of place where you walk through the door, and the doorbell jangles, and everything to do with the subject is there. It puts you right at the heart of the thing you are to do with"

Simon Mottram, founder and CEO, Rapha

Ben steers me through the store at great speed. At one point, I feel his hand on my elbow. "There," he says, pointing at the central aisle. "Down there." There's an insistence to his movements, as if something catastrophic is going to happen if we don't get there quickly.

Like the archivist of some rare and precious collection, he is able to home in on exactly where he wants to go without seeming to have to look. Just a few seconds ago, we were outside in the rain. Now Ben is prying open a cardboard divider and pulling out an album with surgical precision.

"There you go," he says with a nod. "Told you. Great cover, huh?"

I look at it for a moment. It is indeed a great cover; an austere, timeless design with a monochrome shot of the band. It feels reassuringly heavy in my hand.

"Go on then," he says. "Buy it."

And somehow I am on my way to the till, soon to be the proud owner of a vinyl copy of the indie band Savages' new album, *Silence Yourself*.

Now, given that I am not much of a buyer of recorded music, such an impulse purchase is highly unusual for me—and given that I haven't owned a turntable in 20 years, buying a vinyl album is a strange thing to do indeed.

But this is what happens around Ben. It's difficult not to get caught up in his excitement.

We are in Rough Trade East, a music store in London's shabby but achingly hip Shoreditch area that points to the future of retailing in the emerging social and economic paradigm. Rough Trade is not only bucking a trend that has seen three-quarters of the UK's independent music stores close in the past decade, but it is delivering double-digit growth in a time when retailing experts are saying the music store is dead as a viable business.

Ben is 49 years old and has a senior-level job with a telecom company, but when it comes to music he has all the infectious and uncontained enthusiasm of a teenager. The night before, he had taken me to see Savages play at the British Film Institute. It was a short set, the highlight of a night that started with a documentary about the late Australian guitarist Roland S Howard. The event wasn't intended to be a gig so much as a theatrical event—the idea was that we would sit and watch. But as soon as the band came on, Ben had charged down to the front with four other similarly stout middle-aged men and started to gyrate in a way that left most of the crowd—including myself—decidedly uncomfortable. After the first song, the band's lead singer, Jehnny Beth, ushered them to the front and politely asked them if they could sit down. There was much nodding, and within a minute Ben was back in his seat and the show resumed.

"Yeah," he said, leaning back in his chair. "She is one cool chick." He was devoid of any embarrassment. For him, it is all just part of the magic of the evening.

Our trip to the Rough Trade store has the same insistent energy. It doesn't feel so much as if we are on a shopping trip as on a pilgrimage.

While finding the Savages' album took a matter of seconds, the process of getting to purchase it is a whole different ball game. On the way to the till, Ben gets distracted by all sorts of bits and pieces. He is in the process of painstakingly replacing his CD collection with original vinyl, so he spends some time hunting for the versions he is looking for.

"You know, CD was the worst thing that happened to music," he says, waving two albums triumphantly at me. "It took all the fun out of it. I like it that my vinyl has its own unique crackle."

Eventually, we do get to the till. But just as I think I am going to get to purchase my item, Ben strikes up a conversation with the sales assistant about the Savages gig. It turns out they are both fans and they do that thing that fans do—quickly getting into a sort of verbal fencing tournament. It is friendly but highly competitive at the same time, a fine example of the coopetitive nature of fans. By the end of the conversation, we have discovered another favourite band of Ben's are playing at a venue around the corner in a couple of weeks. It's only just been announced, and Ben has to concede a painful point: admitting he doesn't know about the gig in return for finding out where he might buy tickets. This moment of humility brings forth gold as it turns out Rough Trade has just started selling them, and they are going fast.

When the till finally rings up, I have bought one brand-new

Savages album, and Ben has bought two albums, a single, an album-shaped canvas shoulder bag that he is very pleased looks nothing like anything a DJ would ever use, and two tickets to see Big Deal at Cargo. That is not bad for a man who swore he wasn't going to buy anything today.

Rough Trade East first opened in 2007, replacing a much smaller shop farther west in Covent Garden. The Shoreditch store is about 10 times bigger than the original. Since it opened, it has posted growth of 20 percent every year—which would be an extraordinary result in a good market, never mind a contracting one. On the back of this, the company has opened an even bigger store in New York.

Rough Trade's expansion comes at a time when shops selling products that are easy to buy online are closing left, right and centre. In the same month that Rough Trade announced its New York expansion plans, five British retail chains with a combined turnover of £600,000 went into receivership.

Although selling records generates a good chunk of Rough Trade's income, it is not so much a record store as a destination for people like Ben who love indie music. It has its own venue, an in-house DJ and a café, and it sells all sorts of curios and paraphernalia that catch an indie fan's magpie-like eye. It can't compete with the Internet on price for products, but where it wins hands down is when it comes to ambience, human connection and the nuance of a real experience.

Rough Trade is very clear who it is for and what it stands for: "We happily ignore media and industry analyst stereotyping of music 'consumption', focusing instead on the reality, providing independent thinkers with independent music in an independent fashion."

After our protracted purchasing journey, we sit down and get a coffee in the in-store café, and I look around. Even though this is a fiercely anti-establishment crowd, there is a common aesthetic permeating the room—a lot of black, Doc Martens and funky shoes. Vintage clothing is *de rigueur*, as are tattoos. The group is not bound by age. Ben is by no means the only plus-forty-something in the building. Every age group, from teenagers carting skateboards to a man who looks well into his 60s, with a long silver ponytail, roams the store. But they clearly belong to the same tribe.

The reason Rough Trade is thriving is because it isn't a shop, it is a meeting place—a tribal home, somewhere people like Ben feel they belong. It isn't a contrived "customer experience'. It feels real. The experience is as much about the people go who there, and the conversations they have, about the posters, and artefacts, and music the staff have chosen to play, as it is about the fixtures, fittings and digital interactions.

What I came to realise through my travels is that when people with a common purpose and passion gather together, something magical and special is formed. They connect. It is something you can only really experience by being there. It doesn't matter what culture you are in, it is always the same. It isn't something you can see. But it is something you can feel strongly.

It is the thing that we all seek.

When groups of enthusiasts gather together, there is a collective trust. You can't fake authenticity. It is binary. It is either there, or it is not. Fans and enthusiasts have incredibly sensitive bullshit detectors.

In many retail stores, sales assistants are trained and incentivised to try to get people to buy things, whether they are right for them or not. The mentality is to shift product. What is more, they are trained to upsell—to get people to buy more than they really need or want. In Rough Trade, you know that whatever you are told will be honest. A sales assistant is just as likely to tell you an album is a pile of shit, if that is what they think, as they are to tell you that it is the best thing you'll ever hear. Paradoxically, this means people like Ben often come out of the store with more than they mean to. The sales assistant wasn't upselling when he sold Ben the Big Deal tickets, he was sharing something he valued. The result might look like an upsell to a cynic—after all, Ben bought something he didn't originally intend to—but it comes from a whole different motivation: the desire of one fan to help another. It is in this paradox that Rough Trade's stellar sales figures show up. You can let your guard down at Rough Trade, safe in the knowledge that those who work there have your best interests at heart. You know that no one is going to home in on you and say in a fake-friendly tone, "How are you doing?"—an experience guaranteed to send most shoppers' cortisol levels through the roof.

The role of a buyer in a business like Rough Trade is replaced by that of the curator, someone with an instinctive feel for putting together unique and interesting sets of items that appeal to a group of fellow aficionados and fans. The role of a store worker is not to sell but to share passion and knowledge, to help fans find things that will delight them. There is no them and us. Everyone is playing the same game, connected by a common unspoken code and bond.

Rough Trade is a home to a network of fans who identify closely with what it stands for. And fans—even cool ones with an anti-establishment bent—are strongly protective of the things they love. They become highly committed stakeholders in their ongoing wellbeing and success. Ben knows he might be able to get things cheaper online, but he is happy to buy from the store as he knows he is contributing to its success—in fact, he sees it as a matter of integrity. He gets quite angry when I question whether some people might browse the store for albums and then go home and buy them cheaper online: "Not here," he says stridently. "We all know the deal. Enough places have closed. This place is ours, and we want to keep it that way."

Ben's words shed light on what the emerging new economy is all about.

Rough Trade is a beautifully compact and vivid example of how to pivot and build a successful participatory business in the rapidly emerging new economic order, particularly as it was born from an industry so heavily disrupted by digital tech.

In a world where products will increasingly become commodities, where the power of the Internet and digital communications will continually flatten prices, and the monetary value of digital content will tend towards zero, a new economy is emerging that is focused on our higher human needs; our social needs, and what psychologist Abram Maslow rather mysteriously referred to as 'self-actualisation', but might more simply be called our 'spiritual needs.'

Rough Trade demonstrates the three fundamentals shifts required to succeed in this emerging paradigm.

1. It is focused on the why not the what, the fulfilment of a very clear social mission, which it lives and breathes. This isn't some hokey strapline, it is a credo, a promise, its reason to be. It is something that feels deeply meaningful and important to all those involved. This stand is its brand.

2. It is about participation over products. Sure, it sells records and books and t-shirts and all manner of stuff. But like Rapha, its focus is first and foremost on enabling fans to participate more fully in what they are passionate about. The brand and the store might have a vintage and analogue feel about them, but it is essentially a very modern platform business: it connects fans with what they care about, be it gigs, records, books, information or other fans. It isn't about selling products; it is about the whole

human experience.

3. There is no them; just us. Rough Trade acts as a gathering place, a hub, and social connecter for a very specific community that is made up of people who are fiercely independent and individual, but, like all human beings, have an innate desire to feel part of a group they identify with strongly. This generates a deep sense of affiliation, belonging, and ownership for everyone involved. Rough Trade doesn't have customers, it has fans, and as Ben showed, fans are intensely loyal to and protective of the things they love; loyalty, kinship and trust become intrinsically enmeshed.

Purpose. Participation. Belonging.

As we head back out into a rainy winter's day, Ben glances over his shoulder with a look that is fleetingly sad. In a world that is increasingly fractious and fragmented, he is leaving a place that, for him, fulfils one of the most fundamental of our human needs: our need to feel connected.

This is the currency of the new economy, the invisible force that is powering the successful, high-growth businesses, enterprises and movements in the rapidly emerging new social and economic paradigm.

III. How it works

Framework

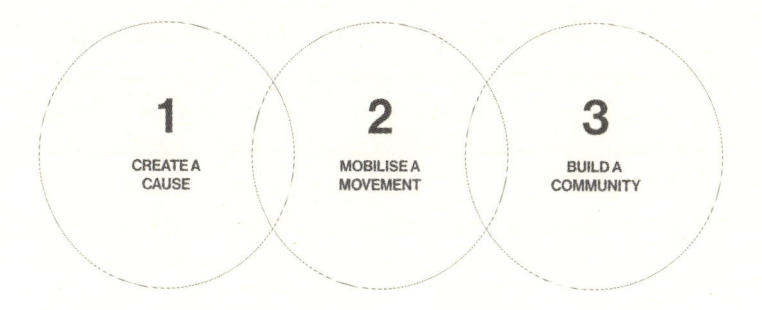

1 CREATE A CAUSE

2 MOBILISE A MOVEMENT

3 BUILD A COMMUNITY

The problem with the body of work that constitutes much modern business, leadership and management thinking lies in its roots. The discipline of Management Science was born out of the Second World War as a means to look at how to optimise the performance of increasingly complex hierarchical organisations in highly challenging times. Since then it has grown in sophistication and complexity, spawning the profession of management consulting in the process. But its underlying DNA has remained the same.

It is like a petrol-engine car. It doesn't matter how complex, clever or high-performing a new model is. The underlying tech is the same.

Bolting a social purpose to a consumer business is like bolting a spoiler to a saloon car. Underneath, it is still a saloon car.

Digitisation does not equal transformation. If you digitise a company without fundamentally shifting its focus, ethos, structure and value proposition, all you are probably doing is speeding up its demise.

To thrive in the emerging new social and economic paradigm requires a radically different kind of thinking, leadership, organisational structure, and way of measuring performance and success.

That is what this section is about. It provides a framework from which new enterprises can be generated and existing ones transformed. It contains case stories chosen to provide insight into how the principles work, and to challenge ways of thinking and operating that in many cases have come to be perceived as truths. And it introduces the beginnings of a new set of measures and metrics to manage performance, and gauge the health and wellbeing of our organisations and wider societies.

1. Create a cause

Principles

- **Make your primary purpose the fulfilment of a social mission**
  Why over what
  On the side of the user
  Singularity of purpose

- **Take a stand**
  Worthwhile and meaningful
  Out to prove a point

- **Innovate in the world of your participants**
  Demand side
  Whole human experience
  Participatory innovation

1. A new kind of leadership

"When I got started, my role models were the semiconductor guys like Robert Noyce and Andy Grove of Intel, and of course Bill Hewlett and David Packard. They were out not so much to make money as to change the world"

Steve Jobs

By the late summer of 1996, it was clear that Apple was in big trouble. The much-publicised launch of its Newton—a product the company had hoped would reboot its fortunes—had been an embarrassing flop. Its inventory had become a confusing mishmash of uninspiring boxes that had begun to look suspiciously like dull corporate PCs, except they cost much more. And its share price was flatlining at the bottom of a deep three-year trough.

As the summer turned to autumn, the company announced that it was laying off one-third of its workforce in an attempt to stem a spiralling cash-flow crisis. It was also putting its much-loved Silicon Valley factory up for sale, a clear acknowledgment that it was in deep trouble.

When Michael Dell, then CEO of the most successful personal computer maker in the world, was asked what he'd do if he were invited to run Apple, he said: "I'd shut it down and give the money back to the shareholders."

Things looked very bleak indeed.

But this is when Apple's board made a decision that, with hindsight, may well be the most audacious a board has ever made—a decision that would not only transform the fortunes of the company, but set in play a series of events that would transform the way the whole world worked. A big assertion, I know, but it really was that profound.

Apple was in dire need of a new operating system for its desktop machines. Its attempts to develop one in-house had become mired in a seemingly never-ending series of hold-ups and missed deadlines.

So, in what many analysts at the time thought was an act of desperation, Apple's board made a decision to buy NeXT, the company that Steve Jobs had set up after he was ousted from Apple back in 1985.

Acquiring NeXT gave Apple a much-needed new operating system to work with—and a really good one at that.

But far more crucially…it also gave it Steve Jobs.

While Apple's engineers were tasked with the job of modifying NeXT's OS to work with its drab grey boxes, Jobs was given the job of turning the company around.

And this is when he did something that would set Apple on course to become the most innovative, influential, and valuable company of the 21st century—and in so doing, pave the way for a generation of new companies that would soon start to transform the way the world worked.

Decked out in his now famous black turtleneck and wearing a pair of alarmingly short shorts, Jobs addressed Apple's employees.

Instead of talking about what you might expect a turnaround leader dealing with a crisis to talk about—a new strategy, new products, cost-cutting, and so on—he talked about something entirely different.

"What we are about isn't making boxes for people to get their jobs done, although we do that very well," he started, clearly talking from somewhere deep within himself.

"Apple is about something more than that. We believe that

people with passion can change the world for the better."

"What we are going to do is get back to that. A lot of things have changed. The market is totally a different place than it was a decade ago.

"But values and core values—those things should not change.

"The things that Apple believed in at the beginning are the same things that Apple stands for today."

And with that he started to show imagery and quotes from leaders and people who had been at the source of profound change: Albert Einstein, Miles Davis, the civil rights activist Cesar Chavez. There was not one product or mention of technology. It was all about *the big why*.

What he didn't talk about—not once—was the one thing that had brought him into the company: revenue. Apple had just shed a third of its workforce. It had sold the factory that Jobs had put a lot of effort into creating and used to talk about with great affection. It had a cash-flow crisis.

But Jobs didn't mention revenue at all to the workforce. This characteristic is crucial. It is easy to think that pivoting a company to focus on a social mission is about doing some workshops, writing some stuff down, putting up a few slides for employees. It is easy to confuse pivoting the company to a social mission with coming up with a new mission or purpose statement. But that is like confusing climbing Everest with buying some new climbing equipment.

Over the course of developing this book, I visited a lot of high-performing enterprises: large, small, high-tech, low-tech, revenue-gushing businesses and not-for-profits; every shape and form. And the most striking characteristic I saw in all the places where there was genuine innovation, energy, and high growth wasn't just that they had a clear social mission, but that their social mission pervaded everything they did. In one way or another, it was all their leaders ever talked about—not as an abstract concept or set of words, but as the essence of why the company existed. This is not to say they were not interested in strategy, execution, cash flow, or any of the many other things that make a company tick, it is just that those weren't the conversations they traded in.

In a time of transformation, when it is not just technology but the whole social and economic landscape that is radically and rapidly shifting, focusing on the why rather than the what isn't a nice-to-have or a noble thing to do; it is the only way to survive and thrive. *Whys* don't change, *whats* do—and fast.

If we apply Moore's law to technologies like solar, blockchain, and artificial intelligence, in the next 10 years we are going to see the total transformation of the energy industry, financial services, and a lot of skilled-knowledge industries like engineering, medicine and law. Remember the Luddites, remember the East India Company…

In 1900, one of London's biggest problems was horseshit… and by that, I really literally mean horseshit. The streets were piled high with dung from all the horses that moved people around. Intricate and expensive plans were hatched to deal with the crisis. Twenty years later, though, the thought of such schemes seemed absurd, as cars, trolleybuses, tube trains and trams had taken over.

Twenty years from now, we may well be looking back on hydrocarbons with a wry nostalgia—cars with internal-combustion engines a niche concern of aficionados and collectors in the same way that vinyl records are today.

In the folklore of start-ups, there is often a focus on the garage they started out in. It is certainly true that Steve Jobs started Apple is his parents' garage, but Jobs and Wozniak developed their ideas and products out in the world of their users in the Homebrew Computer Club in Menlo Park. Their first products were focused on the same social mission that 20 years later would generate the App Store: the means to enable those who were out to change the world, the group of nerds, hackers, hobbyists, and geeks who would go on to build Silicon Valley.

Purpose is the root cause of performance in the new economy. And it needs a certain kind of rebel leadership to inspire people to join a cause. The word "inspiration" has its roots in the phrase "to breathe life into". It also has the same root as the word "spiritual". Steve Jobs engaged at a very deep and personal level. He called Apple "the largest start-up in the world" for a good reason. Under his leadership, its primary purpose was the fulfilment of its social mission. It was all about the why, not the what.

In 1997, Apple was a failing computer company with a rapidly diminishing value of $3 billion. Nokia dominated the high-end mobile phone market. Kodak dominated the photography market. Palm and Handspring vied with each other in the hand-held market.

Twenty years later, Apple's iPhone dominated all three categories. After a spectacular decline, Nokia had divested itself of its failing mobile phone business; Kodak was staggering out of bankruptcy, having totally lost its market share; and Palm and Handspring were long gone.

Apple, meanwhile, had a market capitalisation of $625 billion, making it the most valuable company in the world.

2. Bank to the future

"When I met my wife I was focused on making money, but failing miserably. She taught me that, 'Financial success can never be the goal, only a by-product of living with purpose.' That was a game changer for me"

Adam Neumann, CEO, WeWork

Ravi runs a fish stall in the maze of tiny back streets that connect up the thoroughfares of Pudu market in Kuala Lumpur. His stall is situated on a sliver of a street alongside other stalls packed densely down both sides, each trader's produce bleeding into the next.

Pudu market is a bustling, restless, rabbit warren of hustle and trade. The back streets are particularly frenetic, even on a wet day like today, when the tropical rain has flooded the whole area and everyone has to teeter about on planks.

Pretty much anything that can be eaten by a human being can be bought here, either alive or recently dead, and sometimes transitioned between the two states in front of your very eyes. On the corner, a jolly Chinese man has a pen full of chickens—you choose one, he slaughters it, bags it, and away you go. The stall across the way sells pig's penis among other delicacies. And not to be outdone, Ravi has a big tank on the ground full of thick, black live eels, all straining their necks for air.

Ravi usually works right through from dawn until late in the day, but today being Friday he is closing his stall at lunchtime. For many in Kuala Lumpur, Friday has become a half day—the long midday Dhuhr prayer break leading into the weekend. But for street traders like Ravi, it is just a long break, and he will be back hustling his eels by mid-afternoon.

We head over to the shabbily charming food court at the edge of the market and get an early lunch—you can eat a three-course meal here for less than the price of a mid-sized *latte* at Starbucks in the central malls. I eat chicken *tikka* while Ravi gnaws something off the bone. This is a rare moment of calm in Ravi's frantic schedule. He takes a few moments to talk and laugh with some of the other traders he has known for decades, then we set off through the steaming streets.

The Friday trip to the mosque provides Ravi with an opportunity to drop in at a local branch of Tabung Haji to deposit some money, which is why I am along for the ride. Like many street traders, Ravi deals only in cash, and prefers to keep it close to hand—in the past, stashing it in earthenware pots in his house—so a bank isn't an obvious place for him to go.

But then Tabung Haji isn't just any old bank.

Tabung Haji, or the Pilgrims Management and Fund Board of Malaysia as it is formally known, was set up in 1969 with a distinct social mission: "to provide an appropriate Islamic means of mobilising savings gradually, investing them in economic activities in conformity with *Shari'ah*, thereby assisting Muslims to perform the pilgrimage in Makkah at the least possible cost." Not the snappiest of statements, but very clear nonetheless.

Since its inception, Tabung Haji has maintained this singularity of purpose, focusing on steadily expanding its accessibility and reach, so even poor, illiterate street traders like Ravi have somewhere to save and grow funds. Like most Muslims, embarking on the *hajj*—the once-in-a-lifetime trip to Mecca—is one of Ravi's life ambitions. For him, it is a really big deal. He has never left the city limits of Kuala Lumpur, let alone flown anywhere. So taking a trip to Saudi Arabia is a huge undertaking. It takes years of saving and planning.

Tabung Haji keeps the needs of those it serves very much

front of mind. It doesn't compete with other banks on fancy fads. It's about the whole human experience. It keeps processes and transactions as simple as possible and is continually expanding its retail collection network to ensure it is easy to deposit money. It makes it easy to take out your cash. Ravi is canny and street-smart but has little formal education, so forms and complex processes are something he shies away from. The bank is therefore a model in user-friendliness.

Tabung Haji isn't in the business of money. It is in the business of fulfilling its social mission. But in so doing, it provides a far better return on investment. In the post-global financial crisis era—where capital flows free, and many investors' and business leaders' prime focus is simply maximising the return on their financial investment—what makes Tabung Haji particularly notable is that it has provided its investors with far better returns than conventional banks. In 2012, when many other banks were still struggling, it announced an annual 6.5 percent dividend with a 1.5 percent special bonus, meaning its members got an 8 percent return on a safe investment. And even in the dark days of the financial crisis in 2009, the return was 5 percent. This was far better than most other financial institutions.

Tabung Haji gives Ravi and other hard-bitten sceptics— people who are naturally distrustful of financial institutions— the best of all worlds: their money is safe; it earns a good return, which means they can accumulate more savings and thus embark on their *hajj* earlier; and it is done in accordance with their value system.

In an age when the public perception of the financial services industry has reached a new rock-bottom, and the crazy near-death ride that was the global financial crisis showed an industry that seemed to have lost all contact with reality, Tabung Haji points to the possibility of a different kind of relationship between financial institutions, investors and money, one that in many ways goes back to the roots of why most of them were set up.

What Tabung Haji demonstrates—just as Merck & Co did for much of the 20th century—is that companies and organisations that are driven and led from a genuine and unshakable social purpose not only make the world a better place, but they are far more financially successful and resilient. What it takes is bold leadership, and the ability to have faith and stay true.

The results aren't just a better world and increased profits. They create work and workplaces that feel meaningful, where people feel satisfied and fulfilled. By relaxing the need to control, and letting everyone get on with delivering on the social mission, surly staff become passionate participants, actively engaged. Toxic cultures become creative, healthy, and highly productive environments in which everyone thrives.

We are at the beginning of what is perhaps the greatest period of social and technological change there has ever been, and the disruptive side effects Clayton Christensen predicted are everywhere to be seen—from once-safe businesses and business models to political systems and cultures. Nothing will be untouched.

We all have a choice. We can try and hold on to and maintain social, political, and business mind-sets that no longer work.

Or we can model and join the participatory innovators who are successfully reshaping the world.

As we leave Tabung Haji, I ask Ravi how he feels about his investment. We pause for a moment before we get out into the dusty street.

"It makes me very happy to think about going on *hajj*," he says, for a moment visibly moved. "I have seen the difference it has made in my friends. If I can bring it forward one year, two, maybe even five..." He stops, the thought of his lifelong dream is almost too overwhelming. "I will be very happy," he says quietly.

3. The non-linear business model

"There is a fundamental error in separating the parts from the whole, the mistake of atomising what should not be atomised. Unity and complementarity constitute reality"

Werner Heisenberg, quantum physicist

Complementarity: *noun*
A relationship or situation in which two or more different things improve or emphasise each other's qualities

The economic logic that corporations employed when Steve Jobs set about pivoting Apple in 1997 was a bit like the Microsoft Windows operating systems of the time. On the surface, it looked modern, but underneath it was based on some pretty old tech. Spreadsheets certainly allowed for some slick analytics, but the underlying logic went back 500 years to an Italian mathematician named Luca Pacioli, who, as well as being a Franciscan monk, was a good mate of Leonardo da Vinci. It was a number-crunching model based on classical mathematics.

In the 1970s, a new form of mathematics began to emerge. Quantum mechanics, chaos theory, and systems theory all combined into a new form of non-linear mathematics—a system of logic that underpinned the development of the digital technology and networks that businesses like Apple, Google, Tesla, and WhatsApp are based on. This is the logic of the social economy. It is binary logic, not analogue; it is about holistic systems, rather than granular units.

This is one of the reasons why so many of the successful businesses operating in the new paradigm are led by computer scientists and mathematicians. It is not just the tech that they are immersed in, it is the underlying logic. As computational scientists, Sergey Brin and Larry Page, when they launched Google, understood the concept of "systemic integrity". Either a system could be trusted or it could not. So, for them, their social mission wasn't some sales tool or thing that could be taken or left; it was fundamental to how the system worked.

In the non-linear model, social purpose and financial return are fundamentally entangled with each other, forming a tight correlation. They are like two sides of a coin. They are separate but part of the same thing.

This phenomenon is known as "complementarity"—each part cannot be measured directly against each other, but they are wholly dependent on each other and amplify each other.

Integrity of purpose generates profits. And profit is generated from integrity of purpose. It is a binary proposition; the purpose is either being fulfilled or it is not. If the purpose is compromised, the system breaks down.

In 2015, General Motors wrote this in its annual report: "GM's purpose begins with a few simple but incredibly powerful words: We are here to earn customers for life. Our purpose shapes how we invest in our brands around the world to inspire passion and loyalty. It drives us to translate breakthrough technologies into vehicles and experiences that people love. It motivates the entire

GM team to serve and improve the communities in which we live and work around the world. Over time, it's how we will build GM into the world's most valued automotive company."

In short—and the excerpt was anything but short—it was all about *what* GM did, *what* it wanted, *what* it intended to do. It was a description.

Now shut your eyes. How does it make you feel?

Tesla, meanwhile, was focused on a very big *why*: "Tesla's mission is to accelerate the world's transition to sustainable energy."

That was it. Simple, powerful, worthwhile, meaningful. A cause on which to act.

In 2015, General Motors generated $1.85 on each dollar it spent. Tesla generated $11.

General Motors generated $240,000 of market value per employee. Tesla generated $2.9 million.

2. Mobilise a movement

Principles

- **Enable participation**
  Participation over content
  Tools over products

- **Make it a game—a deadly serious game**
  Coopetitive
  Significant
  Networked

1. Weapons of mass participation

"In dealing all the cards to itself, the system forced the Other to change the rules of the game. And the new rules are ferocious, because the game is ferocious"

Jean Baudrillard

In the introduction I briefly touched on the story of Donald Trump's 2016 presidential campaign. I have to confess this made me a little nervous. No other Western leader this century has provoked so much reaction and division. Using his name has the same effect on some people that catnip and dog whistles have on cats and dogs.

But the reason I chose to include it is that it is a particularly high-profile example of how to build a movement, and how to disrupt an incumbency in the process, even when all the odds seem stacked against you.

Putting the actual content aside, it is the same approach that Arctic Monkeys took to propel them to the top of the UK charts seemingly from nowhere, that Kevin Systrom and Mike Kreiger employed to build Instagram from a start-up to billionaire buy-out in under two years, and Simon Mottram used to create the phenomenon that is Rapha.

It is also the approach that was employed by Jeremy Corbyn when he shook the UK political establishment to the core in the 2017 General Election—so it has nothing to do with political affiliations; Corbyn could not be further away from Trump in personality or political leanings.

Crucially, as the hierarchical command-and-control model of leadership and organisation breaks down, it is the approach that is being used by the high-growth start-ups, disruptors and platform businesses that is changing the way the world works.

So it is worth taking a closer look at how it worked.

On 27 September 2016, Donald Trump stepped onstage in front of a massive crowd of 15,000 people in Melbourne, Florida. About 650 miles north in Raleigh, North Carolina, his rival Hillary Clinton was addressing a crowd of 1,400 supporters at Wake Technical Community College.

There was a little over a month to go in the US presidential election, and Trump was well behind in the polls.

While Clinton laid out her thoughts and ideas, Trump whipped the crowd into a frenzy, encouraging them to whoop, shout and dance. It was something Trump was well-practised at—in previous weeks, he had stood in front of 21,000 people in Dallas, 25,000 in Oklahoma, and 35,000 in Alabama. In the two months since the race had begun, more than 345,000 people had participated in Trump's rallies. Clinton had spoken to 14,000.

Viewed top-down, things didn't look good for Trump: pundits, analysts, and opinion polls all said he was going to lose. Liberal media channels poked fun at his rallies, and a never-ending stream of political establishment figures came out against him, including many in his own party.

But while the majority of the mainstream media, opinion polls and just about every high-profile person going seemed to be vehemently against Trump, something was happening on the ground.

Hillary Clinton was a career politician. Trump, for all his big talk of being an entrepreneur, was most famous for being the presenter of a TV reality game show. This experience turned out to be crucial. Trump was a Twitter user two years before Clinton, and had experienced the participatory nature of reality TV.

He was applying the same tactics that Instagram, GoPro, and Arctic Monkeys had used to appear to explode out of nowhere. He was building a movement from the bottom up. He knew that if you empower fans to participate, they will continue to participate, going out into their communities to share what they experienced. He was mobilising the one percent—the one percent of fans who are highly active in their communities. He was "gamifying" politics.

On 27 October, more than 30,000 people attended Trump's rally in Geneva, Ohio. Two weeks later, with just four days to go before the election, Hilary Clinton went onstage in Cleveland, in the same state. Clinton's team had brought out the big guns—Beyonce Knowles and Jay Z were with her. It was Clinton's biggest crowd by far—18,000 attended. But it was way too late.

What Clinton and her team hadn't realised—just like the music business execs 10 years before—was that a revolution was under way, a paradigm shift. The Democrats were using old-school advertising techniques: coerce people with big-bang emotive content just before the polls, celebrity endorsements, and glamour. It was a top-down corporate approach.

But Trump understood the dynamics of the participation revolution, and he'd had years of experience in reality TV: connect; engage from the ground up; empower participation; get people involved. It was an insurgent, social start-up approach.

Trump's campaign slogan—"Make American Great Again"—was much derided by his opposition, but it was critical to his success. It wasn't simply a tag line, like Clinton's "Better Together." It was a call to action. He knew who he was talking to—the lost, the disenfranchised, those who felt excluded and left out. Join me, he was saying. Participate. Get involved. Make America great again. And they did.

Networks take time to build, but like a fire, there is a moment when they ignite. Trump's timing was perfect. The reason the polls didn't predict the result was because they didn't factor in the network effect. They were using linear mathematics. Causes, though, are a non-linear phenomenon.

Trump built a movement. He enabled participation. He made it a game—a deadly serious game—collaborative, yet fiercely competitive.

2. The Art of transformation

"The world is moving, and a company that contents itself with present accomplishments soon falls behind"

`                                                            `George Eastman, Kodak

"But why?" I asked the CEO.

He stopped and looked at me sharply. "I just told you. Because we are an oil and gas company."

"I know. But *why* are you an oil and gas company?"

His eyes narrowed. It was the look a snake gives to its victim, and that a human being gives to someone they think is being an idiot.

Perhaps the greatest skill of a good consultant is to know where the edge is between challenging and being fired. And I was right on it. I'd been here many times before, but it was never comfortable.

It seems such a simple question—*Why?*—but once we start to tap down into it, it quickly becomes quite hard. Because the question isn't just why. It is *really* why?

It is the question we ask as kids, and the question kids ask us, and often in the moment we realise that we really don't have an answer. "Because…"

Getting to the root cause of *why you do what you do* takes effort. It takes bravery. And it takes work.

The CEO opened his mouth. His brow furrowed.

This was the moment. He looked at his team, then at me again. Finally his face cleared. "You know…that is a very good question."

And so the work began.

We started to tap down. And as we did, the focus began to shift from the *what* to the *why*, from the supply side to the demand side.

Why is the starting point of transformation. In a world where things are changing so fast that if you keep your attention on what you're doing, you get left behind. Focusing on the why creates a context in which innovation can occur.

When we started out, the team was preoccupied with rigs, and drilling and under-performing assets. They had just had their capital expenditure cut by 40 percent and didn't know how on earth they could achieve what they were being asked within such a constrained budget.

When we finished, they were thinking about the energy needs of the region they operated in, about the best and most efficient ways to fulfil those needs, about the profound changes in social sentiment around hydrocarbons and renewable energy.

And they had come up with a why—a very big why. Something that was meaningful and mattered to them, something they could and would stand for.

There is a huge relief in letting go of the idea that you have to know what you are doing. And a really big crackle when you know why. Like *really* why. When it feels right, it touches your heart, lights up your soul, focuses your mind.

We took the conversation out into the enterprise. A critical shift in leadership was required—from telling people what to do, to engaging them in why. It was about emotional rather than operational engagement. This took some effort. It wasn't a philosophy a lot of the team had been brought up with, or a capability they had developed. The correlated nature of purpose to performance challenged a lot of their cause-and-effect conditioning. But we persisted, built muscle.

We applied a different kind of design thinking.

To reiterate the distinctions I made in the introduction, industries that think in terms of "consumers" become preoccupied with stoking desires, and their game is one of manipulation and coercion.

Industries that think in terms of "customers" become focused on their products and services, and how to source, make and sell these.

Teams that think in terms of "users" have a far more human focus, but their preoccupation tends towards the functional. It becomes about tech and interaction.

But placing our focus on the fulfilment of a social mission, inevitably leads us to think in terms of the "whole human experience"—the functional, emotional, social and what might be called "spiritual" needs of those we are out to serve.

And as we did this, things began to shift. Once the focus was moved from what to why, people started to realise a lot of things they were doing could be outsourced, farmed out, and in many cases, just stopped. More crucially, there was a permission and pull to innovate. And once we started to think about the whole human experience, a whole set of new possibilities and innovations emerged. Teams started to compete with new ideas. Young engineers became interested in nurturing local talent in the developing countries the company was operating in, others in reducing the company's carbon footprint through its supply chain.

The company reorganised into three interconnected units: one focusing on maximising the value from its current assets; another on the development of new technologies beyond hydrocarbons; and the third on the transition between the two. At the same time, we took structure out. These weren't top-down silos, but networked communities.

We started to "gamify" the organisation, empowering teams to self-perform.

Purpose and results: these were the measures.

An enterprise start-up was spun out—a lean team that threw away the rule book to develop an under-performing asset. We used this as the means to develop new thinking, creating a sandbox for innovation.

Eighteen months later, the organisation was unrecognisable. There was a buzz and a hum. Teams were innovating. The enterprise start-up model had expanded and started to throw out new cultural, organisational, and technical innovations. Digital tech, non-linear modelling, and AI had become enablers rather than ends in themselves. Whereas before the pull was to follow process, creating complexity and risk-aversion, the coopetitive nature of the new culture encouraged leanness, creativity, agility, experimentation, frugality, and pace—everyone was engaged in the game. People knew what was expected of them, not what they should do.

It is easy to write this stuff down. But like a new diet or exercise regimen, though the theory is simple, the reality is often not. It is messy at times; it takes boldness; it takes faith. We become attached to things, attached to what we do. Letting it go can be hard and painful, which is why we often hang on. At times, the process of transformation can feel a lot like grief. It is difficult and disruptive.

But context changes everything. When we have a big why—something that strikes us as worthwhile, meaningful and important to us—our experience is transformed.

3. Analytics and performance metrics

"Out of this crisis, there could be a rebirth of economics. I'm not someone who would say that all that's been done in the past is terrible. It's just that the models we had were rather narrow and fragile. The problem came when the world was tipped upside down and those models were ill-equipped to making sense of behaviours"

Andrew Haldane, chief economist, Bank of England, 2017

When Andy Haldane addressed the Institute of Government in London in early 2017, he described his profession's inability to foresee the collapse of Lehman Brothers or the ensuing global financial crisis as its "Michael Fish moment"—referring to an infamous incident in 1987 when a BBC weather forecaster confidently predicted that a hurricane was going to miss the UK, only for it to hit the country with full-force the next day, causing devastation and mayhem; the worst storm in a century.

It was a great metaphor. Funny and accurate.

There is a lot to be learned from how climatologists

responded to "The Michael Fish" incident. It changed the game. They started to use and apply complex non-linear mathematical modelling based on chaos and turbulence theories.

This is what is needed in the emerging new social and economic paradigm—to apply the correlated mathematics that Google uses, rather than the cause-and-effect calculations of medieval Italy.

We need to apply new mathematics: non-linear algorithms that look for emergence and the network effect, and the application of computational psychology to understand the often impulsive and seemingly irrational changes of sentiment in highly volatile and dynamic social and organisational networks.

We also need new measures.

The key metric that we have used to measure the performance of our nations for the past 100 years is "gross domestic product (GDP)". This measure ceases to be useful when content and products become devalued, and, in many cases, free. You can't assess the value of open-source software, intellectual crowd-sourcing, peer-based wellbeing, or businesses like Facebook on the value of what they produce.

The key metric of corporations—productivity—is a measure that has been flatlining for the best part of a decade. The reason for this is that it isn't measuring what is driving the new economy. Productivity as a performance metric emerged out of the factory system, where value was calculated by assessing the price of the end product in relation to the cost of the materials, labour, and processes that made it. It was a linear calculation.

Enterprises in the emerging paradigm don't work like that. They are not linear, they are networked. They are complex webs, matrices, and dynamic meshes of interconnections that contribute to the output value in a non-cause-and-effect way.

In the emerging new economic paradigm, purpose is the

root cause of performance. Participation is the means. And the game is the mechanism. These are where we need to be placing our attention. A trinity of KPIs: key purpose indicators, key participatory indicators, and key performance indicators.

In this new model, GDP 2.0—"gross domestic participation"—becomes a far more useful measure of a nation's performance, where the health and wellbeing of a society or company isn't based on what people make, but on how much they participate, contribute, and are involved.

3. Build a community

Principles

- **Facilitate fellowship**
Belonging
Intimacy
Shared experience

- **Empower fans**
Identification
Affiliation
Ownership

1. Together

"It takes time for people to fall in love with you…but it's inevitable"

Ian Brown, The Stone Roses

As we have seen threaded through the stories in this book, connection is the currency of the rapidly emerging new social and economic paradigm. Authentic, real, human connection. It is potentially the most abundant and sustainable energy source on the planet, yet for so many, the most scarce. It is the invisible force that is powering the successful, high-growth businesses, enterprises and movements in the emerging new economy.

As we saw in the stories of Rapha and Rough Trade, in an era where the Internet will increasingly exert downward pressure on the price of products and services, in many cases reducing them to zero, it is the value proposition of high-value brands.

And as we saw in the stories of Stamatis Moraitis and his return to his home in Greece, and John's participation in Alcoholics Anonymous, it lies at the heart of both our collective and individual wellbeing.

It is such a simple concept. Yet it is really difficult to define clearly. What is more it isn't something that can be commoditised, systemised or rolled out. Digital tools can enable connection, as we have seen with WhatsApp, Instagram and Google. But they can also have the opposite effect, as the comments sections of many social media postings attest. The playwright JB Priestley once said "the west end of London is half a million people trying to find each other." Facebook can sometimes seem like three billion people trying to find each other—and often failing. Anger and arguments flare on Twitter. And as many a woeful attempt by consumer brands show, building digital 'user experiences' doesn't mean that people will come.

Fostering, nurturing, and sustaining connection is an art not a science. It takes empathy, patience and care.

This is the reason I built this book around stories rather than processes.

Because the insight shows up in the nuances, subtleties and details.

Which is why it is worth taking a closer look at the story of The Stone Roses. In the Introduction I showed how, by focusing on building a network of fans rather than marketing a product, a band that had been dormant for more than 15 years was propelled from a small free gig in a local town hall to the fastest-selling entertainment event in UK history in under six months—selling over a quarter of a million tickets in just a couple of hours.

In the Introduction we looked at the mechanism. But what is critically important is understanding the power source.

The Stone Roses' original collapse had been attributed to their getting caught up in the studio, making their second album. Their debut had been hacked together as they built their following, in a frenetic period when they exploded onto the scene. It quickly became a classic—and is still included in *Rolling Stone* magazine's top 500. The second album, though, took them nearly four years, a period in which they didn't gig. And when it came out, the Stone Roses seemed to have lost something—the spark that had made the original album so infectious. They embarked on a massive tour to promote the album, but somewhere along the way, band tensions got the better of them, and they folded.

The source of their epic comeback lies in how they reconnected with and rekindled that original spirit.

The first rumours that the Stone Roses were about to re-form started in April 2011. The band's original bass player, Mani, who had always been the group's honest broker, immediately denied there was any chance of a reunion. It looked like just another unsubstantiated rumour blown out of proportion by an industry known for its love of hyperbole.

But this is where a community started to reform. Band members started to talk to each other. Articles appeared in the music press, and, most crucially, conversations were provoked on fan forums. The embers started to glow.

Six months later, though, the band called a press conference. It would be the first time all four of the original line-up had been in the same room since the break-up. In the press conference, they announced that they were re-forming, and would embark on a tour, culminating in two nights at Heaton Park, a venue in their home city of Manchester with a capacity of over 70,000. To those not directly involved, this seemed a ridiculously ambitious goal for a band that had not played together or released any new material for more than 15 years, especially since they hadn't played a solo gig of that size even at their peak.

What these doubters didn't know, though, was what was going on under the surface. Conversations are networks, and the networks were beginning to be built. This is why how the first gig in Warrington town hall was set up was so important. It wasn't about finding a venue and getting people to fill it; it was about connecting with fans and bringing them together.

That first gig was a homecoming, a resurrection; the re-establishment of a tribe—a group of people who shared a deep sense of common interest and connection.

From there, the word spread from fan to fan, pictures went on to social media, stories on to fan forums. It wasn't just that the Stone Roses were back, it was that the vibe was back—that invisible thing we can never truly put our finger on, but know it when we feel it.

As the band started out on tour, they maintained a similar approach—they engaged fans, local radio stations. They weren't aiming at everyone; just the fans who identified closely with them.

And this is where the connection was created, in the conversations, the shared rides, experiences, moments and gigs. Fans trust each other, which is why they are open to what is shared with them. And they are generous, which is why they so readily share with others. There was a vibe in the venues that was difficult to describe, but everyone understood; a deep sense of belonging, of connection to a shared experience, something that was meaningful—and connection is the thing we most need and the thing we most crave. It is emotional "why-fi." When it is there, it is palpable. We feel safe, and home—where we are supposed to be. We feel whole, complete. We feel happy. We can't see it, touch it, measure it, or exactly define it. It is knowingness, a felt experience.

Everywhere that I experienced thriving, growing organisations, I felt it. And everywhere I went where there was stagnation or lack of growth, it was notably missing; there might have been a vision, a change of initiatives, new office fit-outs, diversity programs and employee perks, but that thing, that feeling of connection…it wasn't there.

The ability to build businesses, movements and tools that foster, enable and maintain authentic human connection is the most important, and potentially lucrative, capability in the 21st century.

2. That thing we most seek

"There is no 'them' and 'us.' There is only us"

Father Greg Boyle, Homeboy Industries

Neil Papworth has been a software engineer for 30 years. On the surface, he is a fairly average modern man—with a life spent working for a series of tech companies, more driven by an interest in the technical challenge and steady employment than a desire to set the world alight. When asked about interests outside of work, his first response is curry and beer. Papworth would be your archetypical regular guy, except for one important thing.

On 3 December 1992, he did something that changed the way the world works. Something that makes him perhaps one the most influential participatory innovators of modern times.

In 1991, Papworth joined a company called Sema Group Telecoms in Newbury in the UK.

One of Sema's main clients was the newly founded telecom company Vodafone. Papworth was put on a project to help Vodafone develop a messaging service that would offer pager-like functionality for what would be the new first-generation mobile phones it was introducing—creating the means for users to send a phone number to a handset so the user could call them back. It was a typical example of porting thinking from a previous technology to the new.

On 3 December, Papworth was working in Sema's office when he realised that one of his clients, Richard Jarvis, was at the Vodafone Christmas party across town. Being a good bloke, and perhaps being a consummate professional too, Papworth decided it would be fun to send Jarvis a message. At this stage, mobile phones didn't have keyboards that supported characters.

So Papworth hacked together a message on his PC and sent it to Jarvis's phone.

The message simply said "Merry Christmas".

What Papworth had just done was send the world's first text message. Of course, at the time he didn't realise what he'd created. He wasn't a product designer or marketeer, he was an enthusiast—like Steven Sasson at Kodak—interested simply in playing with the technology available to him to do useful things. All he had wanted to do was delight a friend and client in the festive period.

Papworth's text messaging idea intrigued his fellow engineers and was soon added to handsets as a feature. It didn't cost the networks anything, and it was a nice little add-on, in the same way that early handsets had crude games on them. The thinking at the time was that it might be useful for engineers if they had to test the network. It certainly didn't appear on the radar of those tasked with monetising the new mobile networks. Their paradigm was voice communication, and that is where they focused.

Meanwhile, though, groups of customers who knew each other started to play with texting. It provided the means for them to create small virtual gatherings, enabling them to share and connect with each other in a way they had never been able to do before.

While the new mobile networks vied with each other for customers by spending a fortune on conventional advertising, a completely accidental and far more powerful retroviral process was unfolding between groups of friends. Because texting was only a free add-on, it only worked between users on the same network, so people encouraged their friends to join the same network as themselves so that they could text each other. Whereas the advertising thinking was about encouraging person-to-person communication—in the same way landlines worked—the power of affiliation drew people into networks with groups of friends. They wanted to belong, to take part, to connect with people they knew, and with whom they had something in common. Friends showed each other how it worked. Social groups traded jokes and arranged meetings among themselves. Mobile phone uptake began to spread in these groups like wildfire. Papworth's participatory innovation was doing what retroviruses do, spreading out from small gatherings of enthusiasts with a shared common purpose, not down from the top.

It took the networks' product managers some time to twig that what they had let their engineers add to their handsets as a gimmicky giveaway might actually be a source of revenue. Towards the end of the 1990s, they opened up texting between networks, at the same time charging for it. Because there was so much social cohesion among the established groups, these new charges were tolerated. The upside was that people could then also connect with those they knew who had decided to join groups on other mobile networks. The use of text messaging rapidly began to grow—in a way no one could have predicted. In many ways, this was the first digital social network—organic, decentralised, and dynamic, driven from the bottom up, from groups of enthusiasts, interested only in being part of a social group an interacting with each other.

What started out in 1992 as a simple technological hack by an enthusiast to send a message to a friend, then proliferated through groups of friends enthusiastically connecting with each other, soon changed the way we communicate, opening up a whole new channel of intimacy and mischief. Kids were suddenly able to text each other at the back of classrooms, people could flirt while at work, and the idea that you had to turn up to meet a friend on time went out of the window: "I'll text you when I get there." And on the back of that grew a multibillion dollar business. By 2013, despite competition from a whole host of free messaging services, global revenue from texting was $134 billion.

But this is only half the story. Because something else happened in 1992 that shows a non-linear correlation with the emergence of the social networks that Papworth's innovation kicked off: the crime rate started to slow up. Ever since the end of the Second World War, the crime rate in Western countries, especially in big cities, had been climbing, reaching epidemic proportions in the cities like New York. But in 1992, for no obvious reason that sociologists could put their finger on, it peaked, and over the next couple of years it started to turn down.

A number of hypotheses were subsequently put forward: improving economic conditions, the gentrification of inner-city neighbourhoods, lower alcohol consumption, the removal of lead from petrol. But none of them quite stacked up. When the Global Financial Crisis happened, for example, the crime rate didn't go up. And in areas where there was little or no gentrification the rates still went down.

In 2012 a team lead by Professor Jonathan Klick from The University of Pennsylvania put forward another hypothesis. What Klick's team had noticed was that the downturn in the crime rate correlated very closely with the uptake of mobile phone usage. This included some intriguing sudden dips and spikes in the curves that mirrored each other very closely. Professor Klick's team asserted that it was the uptake of mobile phones that was behind the sudden downturn in crime.

The conclusion that Professor Klick's team drew was that the reason the crime rate fell was because mobile phones meant potential criminal acts could be reported much more easily; potential victims could call the emergency services in-the-moment, onlookers could call immediately from where they stood. Knowing this was possible then acted as a deterrent to would-be offenders. The more mobile phones there were, the bigger the deterrent. It created a sort of crowd-sourced surveillance system.

It was a very logical explanation.

But what it didn't explain was the intriguing sudden dips and spikes in the curves.

And this may be because while Professor Klick's team were right about the correlation, they were looking in the wrong direction when in came to root cause.

The Grant Study at Harvard University is the longest-running study into adult human development in the world. It was set up in 1938 at the university's medical school and is still running today. The study has tracked the lives of a group of men, with the aim of revealing the underlying factors that contribute to their mental and physical wellbeing. Over the nearly 80 years it has been running, the study has generated a wealth of insight and data.

George Vaillant, a professor of psychiatry, led the project for more than 40 years. In 2009, he published his findings.

As you can imagine, there was a lot of data, and the details of the study are well worth a perusal.

However, what Dr Vaillant concluded was that, for all the different experiences, material wealth, and circumstances of those involved, the study had revealed a single, clear theme— that the source of lasting happiness, deep fulfilment, and emotional wellbeing came down to one thing, and one thing only: connection.

That was it.

"Joy is connection," he said. "The more areas in your life you can make connection, the better."

Once you look at the impact of Papworth's participatory innovation, the dips and spikes in the curves begin to make sense. The earliest adopters of mobile phones—and then texting—were young urban people, statistically the demographic with the highest rates of offending. The development of digital social networks started to create a sense of connection and affiliation among people who had previously experienced feeling alone in hostile and isolating environments. As they connected with communities they identified with and felt part of, they rapidly became fans—connecting to people they trusted, and getting others who trusted them involved. Trust is the key word here. Trust is the foundation on which the social economy is built, and it is created in the connections—the social transactions—between each person.

As the 1990s progressed and the use of mobile phones and texting grew, the crime rate continued to drop. The introduction of camera phones, photo messaging, smartphones, and, finally, formal social media has pushed the rate ever lower. If you look at the curves, you can even see sudden dips when more inclusive and immersive participatory technology came on stream. Instead of attacking what had seemed like a hostile environment, young people were able to engage with it using messaging.

In many ways, we can thank or blame Papworth for the rise of the hipster. Text messaging enabled the means to build communities around identity and affiliation rather than geography—it connected people who were otherwise often isolated in a seemingly hostile world.

Connection is the currency of the social economy, and connection is generated in community: intimacy; belonging; shared experience.

Many companies and organisations put a lot of effort into trying to create inclusive high-performing cultures, and spend a lot of money designing expensive intricate 'customer experiences'. The more you try to control and manage people, though, the more fake it gets. And the more fake it gets, the less we connect. This is the issue today in so many corporate cultures. And with many failing brands. It is why shared workspaces are becoming so popular.

You can't design experiences; people have them. What you can do is create the situations in which they can authentically and uniquely happen. You can create the tools that enable people to participate and more fully take part.

During the last week of the 2016 English Premier League season I was sitting in a café in Dakar in Senegal. Everyone was fixated on the TV on the wall in the corner. It turned out that the local Lebanese community had taken to supporting Leicester City, a team of underdogs, who were on the verge of winning the premiership against all the odds. While I was there it was confirmed—Leicester City had won. As it was announced men jumped up, shouting, "We won! We won!" Grown men hugged each other. Some had tears in their eyes.

When I travelled around the AA meetings with John in California, what was noticeable was the use of the word 'we' in the 12 steps and the literature. "We are all in this together," John would say.

When I was with Putri and her friends as they played with Instagram in Indonesia. the word they used was 'we'. We. Together. Us.

'We' was highly noticable when I spent time with Labour activists in the UK election in 2017—when a movement whose leader, Jeremy Corbyn, was supposed to be unelectable, and, like Donald Trump's 2016 presidential campaign, seemed to have the whole of the media against it, shook the political establishment to the core.

It is hidden in plain sight in the name of WeWork.

Neil Papworth's simple Christmas hello message in 1992 may be one of the biggest gifts that has even been given to society—the means for people to deeply, authentically, and intimately connect with each other, to build communities of which they feel part.

3. Social economics

"God used beautiful mathematics in creating the world"

Paul Dirac, quantum physicist

In June 1997, Paul Tollet attended the Glastonbury Festival in England. Tollet was an independent music promoter from Los Angeles who was finding himself increasingly squeezed out of the LA market by big companies with corporate clout. He was therefore interested in the viability of staging musical events outside metropolitan LA, and Glastonbury looked like a good model—it was the biggest music festival in Europe, set in a rural area, and well away from an urban centre.

What he experienced at Glastonbury, though, was something very different from a rock festival. Glastonbury had grown out of a protest movement in the 1970s (the Campaign for Nuclear Disarmament), and while it was heavily focused on musical acts, it was way more than that.

When Tollet arrived, the campsite was a mud bath. There'd

been torrential rain the week before, turning the whole area into a muddy swamp. But rather than deter people, it seemed to have added to the experience. Women followed Kate Moss's lead and wore Wellington boots with cut-off jeans. A huge structure called "Dub Henge" was created—a homage to the pagan Stonehenge circle, made of old VW Beetles and Kombi vans. The toilets were run with solar, so they didn't need generators that might pack up. The festival had a wild tribal atmosphere, with all sorts of different encampments and side acts.

What Tollet realised was that Glastonbury wasn't about the bands, it was about a huge collectively shared experience. Rather than simply watching bands, people moved around and went to workshops, often ignoring acts they weren't that keen on, and hanging out with their family and friends instead. The camp was zoned into different areas, some loud and raucous, others designed for families, some silent, for those interested in meditation. Glastonbury's counterculture roots had flipped the big rock concert model. It wasn't about the acts, but the communities, and the communities within the community. The acts were just an element.

When Radiohead played to 90,000 people on the final night, it had more the feel of a giant pagan festival than a gig. As if everyone was coming together to commune.

Tollet's experience at Glastonbury provided a template for what would become the biggest festival in the world, the Coachella Valley Music and Arts Festival.

The Coachella Valley runs through the desert 130 miles east of LA. The festival is hosted in the small city of Indio, just down the valley from Palm Springs. It is a stunning location. In the day, the sky is a spotless bright blue, and as night falls it melts into beautiful hazy azure.

The inaugural Coachella festival was held over a single

weekend in 1999. It had five major acts and a far more conventional rock festival feel than Glastonbury. About 37,000 people attended.

Very quickly, though, it diversified, taking its cue from Glastonbury, but with a distinctly Californian vibe. In the following years, big bands were augmented by a growing array of smaller acts, arts and crafts, workshops, yoga and more.

By 2004, the festival had added a second weekend and numbers hit 110,000. Three years later, a third weekend called Stagecoach was added, with a distinctly country vibe—and different set of fans, with different interests and preoccupations. The total number of participants over the three weekends soon surpassed 200,000.

The Coachella and Stagecoach festivals have become an intrinsic part of people's social calendars. In a world that is becoming more and more socially fragmented, where many workplaces have become shanty towns of anonymous cubicles, where jobs are high-pressure and there is little time to bond, where shopping malls designed to keep shoppers in a state of high anxiety dot the landscape, and where people are locked away from each other in cars on motorways, Coachella is an oasis in the desert, a place to go and connect—with peers, with tribes, with things people care about and love. It is a place you can be yourself and be with others. A place where people have your back.

In 2015, all 198,000 tickets for the Coachella festival sold out within 20 minutes of being made available online, generating $85 million in immediate revenue.

But ticket sales were just the tip of a revenue iceberg. Whereas consumer economics are extractive—focused on how much value can be taken out of an asset—social economics are generative; they create a ripple effect. Revenue streams become revenue networks. The money spreads out.

In total, the 2015 festivals generated $704 million across a vast network of enterprises that included transportation, catering, hotels, local business and contractors. $403 million went directly to businesses in the Coachella Valley, with $106 million of that going to businesses in Indio itself. Rather than taking out, Coachella put in. The City of Indio generated $3.2 million in additional tax, increasing its available civic budget by eight percent.

Total global revenue generated from the sales of recorded music in 2015 amounted to around $8 billion and was falling fast. The Coachella and Stagecoach festivals generated 10 percent of that figure over just three weekends, with much of the revenue dispersed into local businesses and the community, rather than being concentrated in the hands of anonymous shareholders.

The consumer economic system, especially as it has mutated into its extractive endgame, is, at its heart, miserly and self-serving. It encourages empty consumption. It sucks wealth out of society and concentrates it in the hands of a few. It encourages hoarding. In contrast, the social economic system is generative and expansive.

When you apply non-linear mathematics to the whole system, rather than narrow-view spreadsheet analysis, when you look at the correlations rather than simple cause and effect, they show one very clear point. By focusing on the why not the what, by improving the means by which people can genuinely and authentically connect, the complementarity nature of the system means you don't just make the world work better—you generate and disperse a lot more wealth.

IV. Into action

A call to action

"Through all aspects of society, be it art, design, the financial markets, government, technology or communications, we are witnessing unprecedented global transformation—the result of which is impossible to predict"

Malcolm McLaren, 2007

On 31 October 1517, a 34-year-old social activist called Martin Luther marched to the All Saints Church in Wittenberg in Germany, and nailed a document to the door. Luther was something of a polymath; he was a teacher, he wrote music, he was an activist, and a priest. Luther had a vision. Europe was in the midst of a period of massive social and political upheaval—the disruptive phase of what would later become known as The Renaissance.

Luther wanted change, and had laid out what it might look like in a series of clear points that he had printed using a small printing press, a radical new technology at the time, which was having the same effect as blogging and social media today.

Luther's defiant action had him labelled 'a protest-ant', and so a movement was born. Historically, Luther is seen as a religious reformer, but in the 1500s, religion and society were intertwined. What he was really about was liberation. Small local printing presses were established. Religious texts were translated. Intellectual entrepreneurialism was encouraged. Pamphlets with new and radical ideas were circulated. It set in train the development of a new body of thinking that led to the transformation of northern Europe, creating the conditions for both the industrial and social revolutions that would follow, and from which would emerge the founding fathers of America.

We are now in a period of similarly radical social, technical, economic and political upheaval, the disruptive phase of a new societal transformation.

In the next 10 to 20 years we can expect 70 percent of current jobs to disappear. What the story of the Luddites showed us is that resistance to such change is futile. In the Industrial Revolution it was skilled manual labour that was replaced. In the next two decades it will be white-collar jobs, middle management, and knowledge-based professions.

The same fate awaits a number of industries and corporations. This is the message from the story of The East India Company, a business that once controlled over half the world's trade, but, in just a few decades, ceased to exist.

At the start of the book I included a quote from Jon Kabat Zin: "You can't stop the waves, but you can learn to surf." We can't stop the massive disruptive forces of social and economic transformation, but we can learn to surf them. What is more, we can start to think, act and build for what is beyond the turbulence.

There are many ways the future can go, and how we act today is what will shape it.

At one end of the scale is a dystopian vision in which platform businesses will create a new feudal class, with people having to do more and more for less. In which the burgeoning 'gig economy' becomes a rush to the bottom, creating a dog-eat-dog world where everyone is fighting for an increasingly small piece of the pie. Where big data means we are snooped on, artificial intelligence second-guesses our every move, where power and wealth is concentrated into the hands of a few, and where governments become more and more authoritarian.

At the other end of the scale, though, is a very different possibility—and the reason I set out to write this book. If we act now; if we work together. Then there is a real possibility of the emergence of a new golden era for humanity; one in which technology enables the liberation of the human spirit, hierarchy gives way to dynamic progressive participatory movements, collaboration is balanced with healthy competition, communities are built around common interests and goals, work has purpose, life has meaning, capitalism is generative and businesses are focused on their social impact—a world that really does work for everyone.

Imagine a world where everyone felt deeply connected to a sense of purpose, to a game worth playing, to supportive and like-minded communities. Imagine if we were working together rather than against each other.

It really is possible, on the other sides of the wild waves of disruption.

If that is a vision that excites you, then I invite you to join me. You don't have to nail the manifesto to a door, but maybe Blu Tack it to the wall, stick it on the fridge, or use it in a slide.

Whatever you do, don't wait.

Because it's time.

MANIFESTO

1. Create a cause

- **Make your primary purpose the fulfilment of a social mission**
  Why over what
  On the side of the user
  Singularity of purpose

- **Take a stand**
  Worthwhile and meaningful
  Out to prove a point

- **Innovate on the field of play**
  Demand side
  Whole human experience
  Participatory innovation

2. Mobilise a movement

- **Enable participation**
  Participation over content
  Tools over products

- **Make it a game—a deadly serious game**
  Coopetitive
  Significant
  Networked

3. Build a community

- **Facilitate fellowship**
  Belonging
  Intimacy
  Shared experience

- **Empower fans**
  Identification
  Affiliation
  Ownership

Tool kit

A social system is comprised of a set of conversions, distinctions, rules, habits, practices, technical terms, metrics and measures that together allows us to think, operate and act from a different place.

As I researched and wrote this book I started to build up some of the elements that I saw. This is nether exhaustive nor, probably, accurate. It is a starting point, designed to start a conversation and a collective thought process, rather than to propose a solution. It will always be a work in progress.

I have made the tables below available as an open-source Google doc under a Creative Commons Attribution-ShareAlike 4.0 International license to encourage people to use, contribute, add and share.

Strategic shifts

Consumer economics	Social economics
What	Why
Products	Participation
Them	Us

Characteristics

Consumer economics	Social economics
Built around a consumer proposition	Built around a clear social purpose
On the side of the seller	On the side of the user
Supply-side innovation	Demand-side innovation
Customers	Fans
Brands	Affiliations
Content	Experiences
Consumers	Participants
Competition	Coopetition
Consumption	Interaction
Coercion	Care
Aspirational	Inspirational
Diversity	Unity
Exclusion	Inclusion
Creation of intellectual property	Management of conversations
Obsolescence	Reliability
Experts	Enthusiasts
Advertising	Sharing
Marketing	Advocacy
Industries	Ecosystems
Pipelines	Platforms
Hierarchies	Networks
Loyalty schemes	Clubs
Customer relationship management	Connection brokerage

Consumer economics	Social economics
Data science	Data interpretation
Content strategy	Curation
Trickle-down economics	Ripple-through economics
Revenue streams	Revenue networks
B2C (business-to-consumer) B2B (business-to-business)	B2P (business-to-participant) F2F (fan-to-fan)

Value generation and metrics

Consumer economics	Social economics
Extractive capitalism – what value can we extract from the asset community?	Generative capitalism – what value can we add to the asset community or end user?
Value generated from product/asset/IP	Value generated from brokering connection
Cause and effect business model	Correlated business model
Productivity	Contribution
Gross domestic product	Gross domestic participation

Whole human design

Perspective	Focus
Consumer	Cravings and appetites
Customer	Products and services
User	Functional needs
Whole human	Functional, emotional, social and spiritual needs

Models

Connection = Purpose + Participation + Belonging

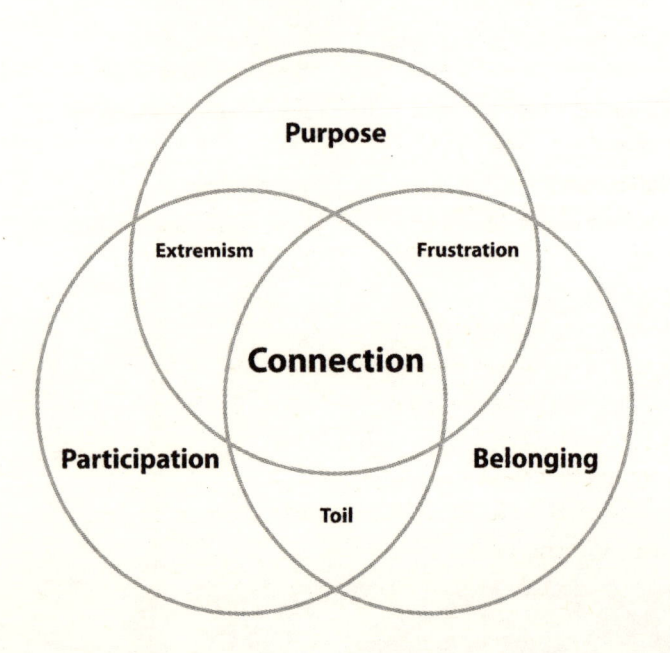

- Purpose
- Extremism
- Frustration
- Connection
- Participation
- Belonging
- Toil